Cullenswood House

*Facsimile of the stamp issued by An Post to commemorate
Patrick Pearse's time in Cullenswood House.*

Cullenswood House

Old Ghosts and New Stories

Edited by
Victoria White

A. & A. Farmar

British Library Cataloguing in Publication Data
A CIP catalogue record for this book is available
from the British Library

ISBN 978-1-906353-13-1

First published in 2009
by
A. & A. Farmar Ltd
78 Ranelagh Village, Dublin 6, Ireland
Tel +353-1-496 3625 e-mail afarmar@iol.ie
website www.aafarmar.ie

Cover design by Kevin Gurry
Printed and bound by GraphyCems

Contents

Buíochas

Ba mhaith liom mo bhuíochas a ghabháil le bord bainistíochta Gaelscoil Lios na nÓg, a thug tacaíocht don leabhar seo, agus do príomh-oide Lios na nÓg, Áine Nic an tSíthigh, a chuir suim ann ón tús.

Táim an-bhuíoch, chomh maith, do an-chuid tuismitheoirí Lios na nÓg. Rinne Yameema Mitha taighde ar na pictiúrí agus táim an-bhuíoch dí.

Go raibh maith agaibh do na tuismitheoirí a thug sean-ghriangrafanna isteach chugainn.

Táim an-bhuíoch, chomh maith, don grúpa tuismitheoirí a chabhraigh linn margaíocht a dhéanamh ar an leabhar, do Geraldine Egan agus June O'Connell a d'eagraigh an grúpa, agus do Mary Doherty ó Red Dog Design Consultants a dhear an leabharmharc fógraíochta.

Míle buíochas, freisin, do Hugh Durham, griangrafadóir Lios na nÓg.

Chabhraigh Caitlín Nic Néilis go mór linn leis an nGaeilge.

Seo chugaibh an leabhar! Bainigí sult as!

Victoria White

Illustrations

Many thanks to the following suppliers of illustrations. The numbers are those of the pages on which the illustrations appear.

Introduction

Victoria White

This book was ghost-written. By 'ghost' I don't mean some poor hack desperate for money. I mean the sort which whisper to you when you go over the threshold of a house and compel you to tell their story.

It was the first time I went up the stairs of Cullenswood House to the semi-derelict upper storey that the ghosts got to me. I had come to discuss with the headmistress of Lios na nÓg, Áine Nic an tSíthigh, what her school could offer my children. More specifically, what accommodation (if any) her school could offer my children.

'Come into the office,' she said, and we both started laughing. The office was a sort of wooden bunker which had been constructed by the parents in the corner of the main upstairs room.

Cullenswood House in the 1990s.

The room had once been magnificent. The sun spilled through the gracious windows. But only a few beautiful, slender wooden bars remained of the frames and there was very little glass. A few off-cuts of wood did the job. It was exactly like a stage-set for an O'Casey play set in the tenement slums of Dublin in the early years of the last century. I thought it was fabulous.

There are some people who are attracted to ruins and I am one of them. Ghosts like ruins too, you see. Cullenswood House before its full restoration was an extraordinary ruin. It seemed like the last piece of Dublin to be saved, and its history just sort of hung there, like the Celtic Revival wallpaper which curled off the walls. I kept feeling, as I worked upstairs on various school projects, that I would find Pearse's diary or perhaps a plan of action from the War of Independence when Cullenswood was a 'safe house'. I kept feeling, in fact, that the ghosts would start to tell me their secrets.

And they did, to some degree. We ran a series of cultural events in the house including a lecture by Elaine Sisson on Pearse in Cullenswood, which was repeated during the Ranelagh Arts Festival. The beautiful big room on the ground floor was full to bursting and the excitement was palpable as Sisson told the incredible story of the founding of Scoil Éanna right where it happened.

She flashed up a picture of a sweet little boy in a St Enda's uniform which she'd found by chance on the web, a certain Euan McGinley. There was a gasp. A woman in the audience recognised him, by name, as her uncle, but she had never before seen a picture of him. There hadn't been time to take many, as he died as a teenager during the War of Independence.

And then there were the Scarletts, relations of the Pearses, who asked could they possibly go upstairs as they had grown up in the house? We were stunned. We asked the film-maker Alan Gilsenan to film them in the house for posterity, and his impressionistic account of the meeting appears here. Éilis Ní Dhuibhne came to address the Irish-language book club and ended up telling us about those far-away days when she was a pupil in Scoil Bhríde and it moved to its bright new building in the gardens of Cullenswood.

So when Mark Leavey suggested to a group of parents that really we should have a book, it had, in fact, already begun to take shape.

I began sounding out the local historians such as Honor O Brolchain, whose own book, *All in the Blood*, had been launched in the house. Our publishers, A. & A. Farmar published O Brolchain's book and so it was the house brought us together; Anna Farmar's brother, Peter Boylan, was also our next-door neighbour in Cullenswood and his incredible patience with the building work had been invaluable. Honor O Brolchain suggested I contact local historian, Sally Corcoran, who in turn suggested the inclusion of the first chapter of Deirdre Kelly's *Four Roads to Dublin*. I rang my friend, the architectural historian Peter Pearson, and found he had fought to save the house and still had his notes from that time.

It really was as if the house was prepared to speak, if we listened. Never more than when, in the later stages of editing, Áine Nic an tSíthigh received a lovely letter from the actress Deirdre Donnelly, saying she had spent her first ten years in the house and would love to come back and visit. We asked her to write a memoir of her time there and her wonderful document of communal living in the 1950s is included here. One member of the 'commune' was an old lady called Rosalind de Cadiz, who Donnelly later discovered had won a medal for her services as a Voluntary Aid Detachment nurse during the First World War. This piece of information identified her as the woman on whom an *Irish Times* letter writer sought information as this book went to proof: with her sister Leila she was a committed suffragette, who served time in prison in London and Dublin for her activities. So now it seems the house can claim a link to another revolution.

Deirdre Donnelly loved growing up in Cullenswood and was only frightened of the ghosts very late at night. She never saw any. But the important thing about Cullenswood is that it makes you think they're there. It is a house which for some reason allows the imagination to take flight. Many of the stories I had heard about Cullenswood turned out to be improbable: Bartholomew Mosse, founder of the Rotunda, was meant to have died in Cullenswood—except that Deirdre Kelly says he died before it was built. Meanwhile, after Pearse's musings on the importance of the spirit of William Lecky to the house, I was surprised to find that there is no evidence that the historian and politician ever set foot in the place.

The essays in this book repeat and contradict each other, and I have deliberately allowed them to stay that way. The stories people tell about the house are as important as any 'truth', which, in most cases, we will never know.

Why do people tell stories about Cullenswood? Is it just the Georgian proportions, the tall windows filled with light? Is it the spirit of its unknown history, the people who were born here, died here, had grand passions and savage jealousies here?

We don't know. But we do know that the house is now here to stay; that it will shelter and inspire the young children who come here to learn; that it will be open, through cultural events, to the people of Ranelagh, and the people from everywhere and anywhere, as a place where they can listen to old ghosts and tell new stories.

Cullenswood: The lands of Cualu

Deirdre Kelly

A thousand years before Richard Crosbie made Irish aviation history, Ranelagh and Rathmines were part of an area south of the River Liffey known as Cualu, separated by that river from what was then the province of Meath (*Mídhe*). Situated beside the ford from which it took its name was the little settlement of Átha Cliath.

To the south, between the settlement and what is now Ranelagh and Rathmines, the land was probably partly farmed, possibly more so at the Átha Cliath end of the area because, for reasons which will be seen later, the other end wasn't too safe.

The main road going through this and leading towards Wicklow was the *Bealach Dubhlinne*, the Dublin Way (through Ranelagh), though from very early times there seems to have been a road to Rathmines and one through Cullenswood to Milltown, part of which is now Mount Pleasant Avenue.

The ancient *Slíghe Chualann* passed along the western border of the area, through Harold's Cross and Rathfarnham. The sea was much closer than it is now with the estuary of the Dodder washing the land not far behind what is now Upper Baggot Street and Pembroke Road.

Barley and grain were at least two of the crops grown close to Átha Cliath. In *Dublin Through the Ages*, the historian Howard Clarke states that 'The ale of Cualu was renowned for its quality' in Gaelic times and no doubt was enjoyed by the early residents of Rathmines and Ranelagh.

By the 13th century most of this land, originally part of the demesne land of the Early Christian St Kevin's Church—and variously known as Colyn, Colon, Cualann—was owned by the Archbishop of Dublin. In the 12th century Archbishop Comyn built St Patrick's Church (later a cathedral) in which he established secular canons with prebends all over the diocese—a prebend is the entitlement of a clergyman to a share in the revenues and a vote in the Chapter (the assembly of the canons). He was succeeded by Henry of London who reserved one of these prebends for himself to ensure that he had a voice in the Chapter. The prebend he reserved was that of Cullen where he had his home farm. The exact location of the house or subordinate manor, to which he retired occasionally, is not known.

In 1172, Henry II of England granted the city of Dublin to his men of Bristol 'to be inhabited and held by them from him and his heirs, with all liberties and free customs which they have at Bristowa and throughout his entire land'. This charter drew many immigrants to Dublin, by then the seat of government with a population large enough to support the many tradesmen and artisans who settled there, and the city prospered.

All was not so well, however, with the native Irish. Dublin had its Merchant Guilds and membership was compulsory for anyone practising a trade. Though large numbers were admitted each year, the Gaelic Irish were excluded as no-one could become a member 'without he be of English name and blood, of honest conversion and also a free citizen of the city'. Norman 'adventurers' brought over by King John, Henry's successor, were pressing ever further into Irish territory, carving up their lands in the Leinster areas of Dublin, Kildare and North Wicklow. All the lands hitherto belonging to Irish chiefs and their tenants were bestowed on the Norman Archbishop of Dublin and on Norman monks and Norman knights.

An inventory of the possessions of the See of Dublin, completed in 1326, gives the extent of the lands of Colon as 1150 acres. The original wood was fairly large, extending to 66 acres. According to the inventory, there were 264 acres of arable land of which 92 were in the plains of Shanballymore. (This seems to have been in the vicinity of St Stephen's Green, possibly the flat lands which stretch from north Ranelagh to the Green.) The old Irish acre varied in size throughout the country. According to a paper read by John Mills to the Royal

Society of Antiquaries in 1889, the acre around Dublin was a little over twice the size of the modern acre, so the measurements given above would be somewhat over twice the size.

Robert Unred, citizen of Dublin, granted '15 acres in Cullen or Colonia to Nicholas of Hattingly' in 1260. It is very likely that these deeds refer to land at the city end of Colon, as land further out would have been under threat from the 'Irish enemye'. The land was rented out, and in 1288 David of Callan rented for farming 'half a carucate of land in the tenement of Collyn' from John the Archbishop. (A carucate of land is the amount of land such as one team of oxen could plough in a season—Chambers *English Dictionary.*)

According to the 1326 inventory, the subordinate manor of Colon appears to have been destroyed. Whether this was caused by Edward Bruce's troops advancing on Dublin in 1317 or by the citizens themselves, who set fire to the suburbs to stop his advance, is not clear. The result, however, was devastating. The inventory lists

> a hall with stone walls now prostrate, a chamber for the Archbishop with a chapel annexed, the chamber roofed with shingles . . . a kitchen formed of wood, a grange, a stable and granary . . . all now totally prostrate to the ground. The meadows, which extended along the highway, were destroyed by the carriers and their horses.

Fifty acres (125 modern) of arable land were sown in wheat and 48 (120 modern) with oats, while 68 (170 modern) lay fallow. The pasture was useless as 'the greater part of the pasture is near malefactors'.

Driven from their homes in the rich lands around Dublin, the Irish entrenched themselves in the wild, barren, natural fastness of the Dublin and Wicklow Mountains. These mountains stretch in an almost unbroken range from Dublin to Carlow. Like a blue backdrop they close the vista of almost every street and avenue leading southwards. There are days when they seem to stand almost behind the buildings at the end of Ranelagh and Rathmines Roads.

The view of Dublin city from those same mountains was equally clear and, as the 12th century drew to a close, the eyes that watched the city were not friendly. United in their hatred of the usurpers of their land, the O'Tooles, the O'Byrnes and other Leinster septs plotted war on the citizens of Dublin as they watched the keep and walls of a great castle rising on the place where their forefathers, the Uí Dunlainge, had their defensive rath. They awaited their opportunity and one Easter Monday, c. 1209, they wreaked their revenge in a bloody slaughter known to history as the Massacre at Cullenswood.

The massacre at Cullenswood

On that Easter Monday morning God was in his heaven and all was right with the world, or at least in the world of those lucky enough to be citizens of the city which was now the centre of Anglo-Irish power. By then the new settlers were well entrenched. Their legal rights were established by charter, the city's boundaries were defined and now stretched south to the Dodder, east to Poolbeg, west to Kilmainham and north to the Tolka. Merchants were protected from competition as a foreigner could not even sell drink in the city, only on his own ship. St Patrick's Church, rebuilt in 1191 by Archbishop Comyn, was soon to become a cathedral and master craftsmen were engaged in the rebuilding of Christ Church.

It has been said that, had the Wicklow Mountains not existed, the history of Ireland might have read very differently, and the events on that Easter Monday provided one of the first incidents of the truth of that statement.

What must have amounted to a large proportion of the citizens of Dublin, which was then probably not much larger than present-day St Stephen's Green, prepared for a day of festivities and sport in Cullenswood, not far from the city. One party of citizens had challenged another to a game called 'Hurling of Balls', a sport which the Bristolians are said to have introduced. According to Stanihurst's account, 'a false brother gave notice of the citizens' intentions to the enemy'.

Even without any notice, the jostling procession of hundreds of people would have been seen from the mountains as they wound their way from the walled city past St Patrick's and St Brigid's churches, converging at Kevin Street and turning south at what is now Camden Street (St Kevan's Port). Maybe they stopped to drink from the holy well of St Kevin, close to Protestant Row (part of the original road to Donnybrook), and continued into Cullenswood, probably by way of Mount Pleasant Avenue which was the 'Highway to Cullenswood'.

Where they stopped to enjoy themselves is a matter for conjecture, since no written record of the day's events has survived. Some have placed it in the area between Upper Rathmines and Beechwood, known as the 'Bloody Fields', though it is more likely that this name refers to the scene of the later 'Battle of Rathmines' in 1649. Probably it was the area between what is now the Grand Canal and Mount Pleasant Square, along the banks of the Swan river which at this low-lying point would have been wider and swampy, particularly at that early part of the year, making the crossing a messy business for so many people. The woods probably began quite close to this point, so the revellers, unarmed as they are said to have been, would not have ventured too far into the area where the 'Irish enemye' lurked.

It seems strange that such a large group of citizens then engaged on building, at great expense, strong walls around their city to keep this enemy out should venture so far from the protection of that city without being armed.

Few survived to see the results of that oversight. The settlers sported and relaxed, little knowing that in the woods beside them the enemy lay in wait. At an opportune moment the Irish broke from cover, the O'Byrnes, the O'Tooles and other dispossessed tribes, slaying all before them. The woods of Cualann must have rung with the shrieks of terror and revenge and the little Swan river (if that was the spot) must have run red with blood, as 500 citizens are said to have died in the massacre.

The annals of Dublin show that it was not forgotten. For centuries afterwards, on Easter Monday or 'Black Monday' as it was later named, the citizens commemorated the massacre by marching with the Guilds of the city, in battle array, displaying a black banner to show defiance to their mountain enemies. The custom must have lapsed at some point as in 1655 the Mayor, Mark Quine,

> revived the ancient custom of marching from the Tholsel to Cullenswood on Easter Monday . . . The brethren and their servants from 16 to 60 years of age were summoned to muster at 7 in the morning, fully armed and equipped

and there are frequent entries in the journals as to these parades and their cost, which in 1656 reached the sum of £55 7s 6d. On one such occasion an anniversary feast was eaten under guard so that 'the mountain enemye dareth not attempt to snatch so much as a pastry crust from thence'.

In 1316 David O'Toole and his clansmen laid an ambush in the wood of Cualann hoping to repeat the massacre of 1209. This time, the citizens, headed by Sir William Comyn, 'fought and chased the O'Tooles for six leagues, slaying 17 and wounding many desperately'.

In 1429, Sir John Sutton, Lord Lieutenant of Ireland, made a successful incursion into the stronghold of the O'Byrnes, for which the Sheriff of Wicklow was ordered 'to provide 100 carts of victuals, bundles of wood, 800 men with axes, 100 men with iron tools and 200 with caltrops'. (Caltrops were instruments armed with four spikes so arranged that one always pointed upwards to obstruct cavalry or a raiding party.) The citizens were obviously chasing what they considered a very formidable enemy.

The existence of 15 miles of mountains, traversed only by pathways, and situated so close to the seat of power, delayed for a long time the establishment of English rule in Ireland. Cullenswood must have resounded to many attacks and ambushes, situated as it was between Dublin Castle and the mountains.

Great must have been the rejoicing in the Castle in 1599 when the head of Phelim O'Toole, owner of the lands of Powerscourt, was presented to Queen Elizabeth by Richard Wingfield. His reward was the manor of Powerscourt and land 'five miles in length and four in breadth . . . fortified by the said Brian and Phelim O'Toole and their heirs'. In the early 17th century most of the lands of the O'Tooles was parcelled out in grants. Small wonder then that the battles, the ambushes and attacks from these Irish septs continued even as late as the 1798 rebellion where Wicklow was a rallying ground for Michael Dwyer and his 'mountain men'. This old ballad gives a sense of the situation through the ages:

Border Forays

There's not a turlough, tarn or dell
From Glen MacArt to Harold's Cross
From Delganie to Crumlin Moss
But each its tale of blood could tell
Of fight and foray, cattle ta'en

And dungeons sacked and burned as well,
When Talbot's spears or Plunkett's men
Dashed in a foray up the Glen;
And blazing rick and burning roof
Told where the children of Imayle
Had flashed like lightning through the Pale
And beacons lit, and hurrying out
Of Marchmen keen, and trumpet calls,
And burghers hastening to the walls,
And banners on the towers displayed,
Proclaimed how ill Clan Dublin liked
Thro' guild or ward, Clan Rannel's raid.

Today there are still many O'Byrnes and O'Tooles in Wicklow and in the last century a well-known character was the 'King O'Toole', who lived in the mountains in a hut. Whenever he got drunk he would hammer on the doors of Powerscourt House shouting 'Leave my house, youse usurpers and imposters', and was just as regularly fined a shilling by the Resident Magistrate, Lord Powerscourt himself.

Extract from Four Roads to Dublin *by Deirdre Kelly, The O'Brien Press Ltd.*

Beatrice Elvery's 'Íosagán'.

How to make an Irish boy: The founding of Scoil Éanna in Cullenswood House

Elaine Sisson

Beginnings

It is a curious experience to stand in the front classroom at Cullenswood House. The gracious Georgian proportions—large windows and high ceilings—are somewhat at odds with the miniaturised tables and chairs organised in neat configurations. The room is not haunted by the past—the faded voices are not plaintive—but the figure of Patrick Pearse is definitely present.

What first inspires a person to start a school? It requires a jumble of ingredients: courage, vision, foolhardiness and sheer determination in the right amounts. To those who knew him it was not surprising that Pearse should decide to open St Enda's as a day and boarding school for boys in 1908. Education had long been a major preoccupation in his teaching work for the Gaelic League and in his journalistic writings, certainly since he became the editor of *An Claidheamh Soluis* in 1903. He was unhappy with the type of schooling he and his brother Willie had received: an uninspiring, rather brutal inculcation by the Christian Brothers. Fundamentally he believed that there was a better way to educate Irish children: that an Irish-centred, child-focused curriculum could be truly transformative—for the child, for the teacher, and ultimately for the nation.

St Enda's at Cullenswood House

St Enda's first home under Pearse's stewardship was at Cullenswood House in Ranelagh. The house was associated with the childhood of the historian William Lecky but it was the grounds to which Pearse was particularly drawn. 'Cullenswood House,' he writes, 'has memories of its own.'[1]

Behind the house there was a spot where 200 years previously the Wood of Cullen sheltered Irish rebels. It was from those woods that 'the Irish, come down from the mountains, annihilated the colonists of Dublin on Easter Monday, 1209 . . . and [where] the fields on which our schoolhouse looks down got their name of the Bloody Fields.'[2]

While Lecky's connection with Cullenswood House gave the schoolhouse a tradition of scholarship, the surrounding lands hinted at a darker and more revolutionary connection to the past. Desmond Ryan, an ex-pupil, noted some years later that the school grounds were associated with 'violent scenes and battles of the past, and with the most sheltered and peaceful scholarship, and then again with the cultural and political movements of the day.'[3]

Pearse was determined that the school would be of a good quality, pleasing and respectable. His interest in the grounds was not limited to bloody histories: he firmly believed in the crucial role of nature and of the outdoor life in the spiritual and moral well-being of his pupils. In the 1909 prospectus special attention is drawn to the school being situated 'in the healthiest part of the southern suburbs' and a section is dedicated to describing the opportunities for teaching nature study, botany, horticulture ('practical gardening and elementary agriculture'), geology, geography and, of course, sports. If he wished, a boy was given an allotted plot of ground which, 'under skilled direction' 'he is at liberty to plan out and cultivate according to his own taste.'[4]

The gardens covered an area of five acres and included an orchard, flower and vegetable gardens, fruit grounds, greenhouses, conservatories, vine and peach houses and 'all the other conveniences

1 *An Macaomh* Vol 1 No 1 Midsummer 1909
2 Ibid.
3 Desmond Ryan 'St Enda's—Fifty Years After' *University Review* Vol II, (1958)
4 St Enda's prospectus 1909

St Enda's hurling team 1909–10. The romance and history of hurling was an integral part of Pearse's vision for St Enda's.

of a well-equipped country mansion'.[5] Apart from the agricultural gardens the grounds included playing fields, a handball court and an open-air gymnasium.

Cullenswood House was impressive in size and structure. Pearse refers to it proudly as 'one of the noble old Georgian mansions of Dublin, with an old garden full of fruit trees under our windows, and a hedgerow of old elms [and] sycamores.'[6] Apart from well-equipped and colourful classrooms and neatly laid-out gardens it boasted a science laboratory, a play room, three dormitories, an infirmary, and, with a nod to progress and modernity, fully certified 'sanitation' and 'a handsome new lavatory'. Pearse was confident that the school could hardly offer more in the way of modern equipment and facilities, except perhaps a special room for vocational and technical instruction.[7]

5 'St Enda's School Gardens and Pleasure Grounds' *Irish Gardening* Vol VI No 60 (February 1910)

6 *An Macaomh* Vol 1 No 1 Midsummer 1909

7 Ibid.

Art and Cullenswood House

Patrick's father, James Pearse, had earned his living as a monumental sculptor—his High Altar for the Rotunda won an award at the 1882 Dublin Exhibition. He had passed on his interest in art and in craft to his children. The collection of pictures, maquettes, and casts of sculptures, as well as the wide variety of beautifully illustrated books currently held by the Pearse Museum, bear witness to Pearse senior's appreciation for illustration, engraving, painting and sculpture.

Willie was especially artistic, studying art in London and Paris as a young man and training under Oliver Sheppard in Dublin. The Pearse brothers fostered a real and abiding interest in art and were determined that Cullenswood House would 'encourage the boys in a love of comely surroundings', and would be fundamental 'to the formation of their taste in art'.[8] Their commitment to providing an aesthetically pleasing environment is evidenced by the number of artists working within Celtic Revivalist traditions who admired the work of St Enda's and contributed their own work to the school.

Artworks which complemented the school's promotion of Celtic boyhood included two symbolist paintings by Beatrice Elvery (later Lady Glenavy): 'Éire Óg' and 'Íosagán'. The first of the paintings 'Éire Óg' was given as a gift to the school by Maud Gonne MacBride. In her autobiography Beatrice Elvery recalls that she 'had painted an allegorical picture . . . of Cathleen Ní Houlihan' with a young child on her knees 'shadowed by a ghostly crowd of martyrs, patriots, saints and scholars.' 'Some time later,' she writes, 'I met one of the boys from the school and he told me that this picture had inspired him to die for Ireland!' Elvery admits to being 'shocked at the thought that my rather banal and sentimental picture might, like Helen's face, launch ships and burn towers.'[9]

The second of Elvery's paintings, 'Íosagán', held a special meaning for Pearse. The painting, now in the Pearse Museum in Rathfarnham, is a pastoral setting of the Christ Child. Set against two sturdy

8 St Enda's prospectus, 1909
9 Beatrice Elvery *Today We Will Only Gossip* London, 1946, p. 91. The painting is now in private ownership but is currently on loan to the Pearse Museum, Rathfarnham.

Beatrice Elvery's 'Éire Óg'.

apple trees, Íosagán stands with arms spread out, as if anticipating crucifixion, while a small rabbit and a bird idle at his feet and lambs feed undisturbed in the background. The inscription, in Gaelic uncial script, is adapted from St Luke's account of the childhood of Christ, and reads (in translation): 'And the Child grew and waxed strong; full of wisdom and the Grace of God was with him.'[10]

Pearse had first published a short story called 'Íosagán' in 1907 in which the Christ Child appears in the West of Ireland. In 1908 'Íosagán' and other stories were published as a collection for which Beatrice Elvery did the illustrations.

Cullenswood House also boasted a stained glass window from Sarah Purser's An Túr Gloine. The panel which was at the front door depicted a triad of candles to illustrate truth, knowledge and wisdom. George Russell donated a mystical symbolist picture 'The Sword of Light' featuring a young couple peering into a Celtic Twilight. Jack Yeats contributed a pen and ink drawing 'The Man that Buried Raftery', executed in 1900 and either bought by, or given to, Pearse for the school. Raftery, the blind Connacht poet, had died in 1835 but the story of his life and his many compositions were well known

10 Luke 1:80

[17]

Group photograph of the boys outside the front door of Cullenswood House.

in nationalist circles especially after Douglas Hyde published *Songs Ascribed to Rafterty* in 1903.

The Yeats drawing went missing from St Enda's after 1916. A few years ago, when Pat Cooke was the curator of the Pearse Museum, he saw the drawing in a fine art auction room and purchased it with the aid of friends of the Museum. It now hangs in Pearse's study at the Hermitage in Rathfarnham. Jack Yeats also designed a Christmas card for St Enda's featuring an Irish lullaby collected by Pearse and later published in *Songs of Sleep and Sorrow* which he published in 1914. The card, printed by the Cuala Press, is a Yeats illustration of the poem 'Cronán Mná Sléibhe' ('Lullaby of a Woman of the Mountains').

Internationally acclaimed designers from Belfast, the Morrow brothers, who were personal friends of both Jack Yeats and of Sarah Purser, were commissioned to design friezes executed in ancient Irish script to run throughout the rooms in the building. A past pupil, Milo McGarry, recalls that the classrooms were decorated with the names of famous Irishmen from Colmcille to Eoghan O'Growney.[11] The Morrows also illustrated a panel of Cúchulainn taking arms as

11 Milo McGarry 'Memories of Sgoil Éanna' *Capuchin Annual* 1930

a young man and inscribed with Pearse's personal motto: 'I care not though I were to live but one day and one night provided my fame and my deeds live after me.' Sadly, the Morrow friezes and panel along with Purser's stained glass were stolen when Cullenswood House was vandalised during the 1960s and their whereabouts are unknown.[12]

The curriculum at Cullenswood House

In his writings, Pearse very clearly sets out his influences for the model of St Enda's. Inspired by the ancient Irish system of fosterage—where a boy is sent from his family to live with intellectual and spiritual mentors—Pearse drew analogies between the pre-Christian or bardic system, the early Christian monastic tradition, and contemporary ideas of education which were beginning to emerge in the work of Maria Montessori and through the influence of Fredrich Froebel. What these models had in common, according to Pearse, was 'freedom for the individual' which sought to 'discover the hidden talent that is in every normal soul'.[13]

Teaching and the role of the teacher as mentor were central to Pearse's philosophy. His desire to found his own school was driven, in part, by the attraction of new teaching methods (especially in bilingualism) but also by the wish to secure 'a genuine Irish education' for Irish children. Pearse's insistence on an 'Irish' school highlights the failure of contemporary schooling to meet the educational needs of nationalist boys. Pearse was uninterested in the existing educational system which churned out boys for employment without any real feeling for their own history, culture, geography or language. The radically progressive nature of Pearse's vision focused on a system in which the child himself was paramount—not child as civil servant or as exam result. In a 'true' education system, argued Pearse in *The Murder Machine*, 'love of beauty . . . love of books . . . love of knowledge . . . and love of heroic inspiration' would be embedded within the curriculum.[14]

The first prospectus of 1908–9 outlines, even by today's standards,

12 The Pearse Museum in Rathfarnham has reinstated the Cúchulainn motto in the style of the Morrow friezes.
13 'The Murder Machine' *Collected Works of P. H. Pearse: Political Writings and Speeches* p. 27
14 Ibid.

A scene from The Lost Saint *by Douglas Hyde, acted by the boys of St Enda's.*

a modern, intellectually engaging curriculum and the school annals of 1908–9 confirm that the curriculum, as promised, was delivered. Denis Gwynn, an ex-pupil, has written that the 'exceptional reputation' of Thomas MacDonagh at Rockwell College meant that many parents, who might otherwise have been doubtful about Pearse's experience, were happy to send their sons to St Enda's.[15] The academic standards of the school are evidenced by the qualifications and expertise of the teaching staff and the large number of professors and scholars who visited as part of a lecture series.

Among the speakers who came to talk to the boys were experts in phonetics, French and German literature, medieval Irish literature, botany, topography, archaeology, Irish history, philosophy, classics, and physical science. In addition the boys were offered a variety of choices: music (choral singing, harp, violin, piano, and uileann pipes); drawing, modelling and practical carpentry; shorthand, typing, book-keeping; dancing, physical drill, elocution, German, French, Spanish, or Italian, and for senior boys Latin, Greek and medieval Irish.

The combination of an inventive curriculum and an active, imaginative input from writers, artists, scholars, linguists and dramatists

15 Denis Gwynn 'Thomas MacDonagh' *Cork Examiner*, 23 November 1967

meant that the quality of the education was far higher than that of the average Irish classroom. The cultural and social engagement at St Enda's with ideas of nationality, language, history and public service disguised a more fundamental, but perhaps more abstract, deliberation on the nature of citizenship: how is an Irish boy made?

For most parents, St Enda's was an opportunity to provide their sons with a good quality, broad-based education, a chance to learn Irish and Irish games and customs and a feeling that they were supporting something worthwhile. By the end of the first year Pearse noted that 'nearly every boy in the school is the son or brother or nephew or cousin of some man or woman who is graving a mark in the history of contemporary Ireland.'[16] Certainly the roll call was drawn from some of the illustrious nationalist families in Ireland. Among them were Eoin MacNeill's three sons and a nephew, and the MP and Gaelic Leaguer Stephen Gwynn's son Denis; William Bulfin's son Éamon attended as a boarder as Bulfin lived in Argentina working as the editor of the Gaelic League newspaper *The Southern Cross*; George Moore's nephew Ulick attended as did W. P. Ryan's son Desmond, later to be Pearse's first biographer. James Larkin's sons joined later in the school's history, while relations of Agnes O'Farrelly, Mary Hayden, Stephen Barrett, Seán T. O'Kelly, and Padraic Colum also enrolled.

The Cullenswood Years 1908–1910

The first year at Cullenswood House was marked by Pearse's determination that the students should be part of the cultural community. By the first two months of the first term the boys had already been visited by most of the high profile cultural and nationalist leaders of the day; visitors included Maud Gonne MacBride, Ella Young (writer and illustrator), Douglas Hyde (President of the Gaelic League), Edward Martyn (founder of the Palestrina Choir), the head of St Pieter's College, Belgium, and, most exotically, a party of Egyptian students brought to visit by Mrs N. F. Dryhurst, a prominent English suffragist. The same Mrs Dryhurst also brought the Gifford sisters to visit—Sydney, Grace and Muriel—two of whom later married Rising leaders connected to the school. Memorably, Joseph Plunkett married

16 *An Macaomh*, Vol I No 1 Midsummer 1909

Grace Gifford on the eve of his execution while her sister Muriel married Thomas MacDonagh in 1912.

Over the two years that St Enda's was based at Cullenswood House a steady stream of luminaries, intellectuals and eccentrics came to speak to the boys. The visitor list reads like an honours roll of the literary revival: among those who came were the writers George Moore, Ethna Carbery, Pádraic Colum, Séamus MacManus, W. B. Yeats and Standish O'Grady; university professors Eoin MacNeill, Agnes O'Farrelly and Mary Hayden also visited; public figures such as Roger Casement, Shane Leslie, Stephen Gwynn, the Hon. William Gibson, paid their respects as did cultural revivalists and nationalists including Margaret Hutton (whose translation of *An Táin* was used as a text book) Count and Countess Markievicz, as well as journalists D. P. Moran and W. P. Ryan, and Dora Sigerson and her husband Clement K. Shorter (editor of the *Illustrated London News* and *The Tatler*).

Some visitors, like James H. Cousins, a poet, playwright, actor and theosophist, embodied the kind of eclectic and creative energy characteristic of the more bohemian aspects of Revivalism. There was unlikely support from international figures too: Rabindranath Tagore, the Indian nationalist; Lord Baden Powell, the founder of the Boy Scout movement in England, and Lord Alfred Douglas (Oscar Wilde's Bosie) were all aware and admiring of St Enda's. Indeed, Tagore established a similar school in Bengal, which was referred to by Yeats as 'the Indian St Enda's'.

The influence of Revivalism is seen most visibly in the dramatic and theatrical productions of the St Enda's boys. St Enda's boys were a regular fixture in Dublin's social and cultural life in the early years of the 20th century. Between 1908 and 1910 the boys performed in Irish language plays at the Abbey Theatre and numerous others in the school. They also acted in open-air pageants of Irish history in the gardens of Cullenswood House, at Jones' Road (now Croke Park) and *feiseanna* around the country.

However, a larger cultural influence is also evident in the promotion of Gaelic games for boys, the recognition of the need for an Irish contemporary popular literature in the form of boys' adventure stories and juvenile tales, and the distribution of many images of the boys at work and play which were sold as picture postcards. The sense that

Con Colbert exercising some St Enda's boys c. 1910.

St Enda's represented the future of Ireland is reiterated by those who watched the boys perform in plays at the Abbey and in the colourful and publicly attended pageants on mythology and history, and saw them marching through the city in the costumes of ancient Ireland. It is also reported by those who bought pictures of the boys dressed as Cúchulainn, admired their skill at hurling and Gaelic football, and watched them drill in military formation in the uniforms of the Fianna Éireann.

The end of an era

By 1910, the size and success of the school meant that new premises were necessary and the school moved to the Hermitage in Rathfarnham (now the Pearse Museum). However, that optimism was shortlived and the years in the Hermitage in Rathfarnham were characterised by bad financial planning, falling numbers and an increasingly volatile climate. Five of the fourteen leaders executed for their part in the 1916 Rising were connected to the school: William Pearse, Joseph Plunkett, Thomas MacDonagh and Con Colbert, and of course Patrick Pearse himself. In hindsight, the Cullenswood years of 1908–10 were the most successful and happy years for the school and for Pearse. The early years are not marked with the level of militarism which was in evidence at the Hermitage.

A large number of boys who attended St Enda's emerged years later in the public service of the new state: they served in the diplomatic corps and the army, worked as teachers and university professors, as doctors, journalists, writers and lawyers. Many maintained a commitment to the arts: Patrick Tuohy became a renowned painter, and Norman Reddin was involved in the founding of the Gate Theatre in 1928.

Today, Pearse is seen as an historical figure, naïve, even dangerous, in his espousal of martyrdom and self-sacrifice; a champion of a Catholic and Gaelic Ireland which contemporary society has gradually and gratefully shed. Certainly, for modern parents the sight of children singing nationalist songs and marching in military formation would be uneasily viewed through the lens of the legacy of European youth fascist movements. However, Pearse's writing on the role of education in defining society has much to offer an Ireland that is currently struggling to articulate what type of society we have developed. A close reading of his writings on education reveal him to be surprisingly modern and pragmatic. In fact, much of what we understand to be Pearse's blueprint for a Catholic and Gaelic Ireland derives, not from Pearse's writings, but from the early years of a xenophobic and conservative nation state.

After his death, Pearse's challenge to reform the Irish education system was thwarted by poor vision, bad management and a narrow interpretation of what it meant to be Irish. Today, the reinstatement of Cullenswood House as an Irish-speaking school does more than any state-led commemoration to honour the legacy of Pearse the educator.

'Too much in the suburban groove'?
Cullenswood, Patrick Pearse and the ideal
Irish school garden

Finola O'Kane

Desmond Ryan, a pupil of Pearse's, wrote in his memoir *Remembering Sion* that Pearse had 'lived and died to realise his three wishes: to edit a bilingual newspaper, to found a bilingual secondary school, and to die as leader of a revolution to establish an Irish republic.'[1] In September 1908, Pearse achieved the second of these aims when he opened a bilingual secondary school for boys at Cullenswood House, an old Georgian mansion situated in the heart of Dublin's prosperous Victorian suburbia.

A large and comfortable house, Cullenswood's heart lay in the 'large square class-room with the names of famous Irishmen from Colm Cille to Eoghan O'Growney inscribed on the frieze'. Bustling through the generously proportioned rooms with Pearse went 'the alert figure of Thomas MacDonagh, vivacious and busy with plans and timetables'.

Pearse attached significance to all his actions, mostly as an afterthought, yet slowly building to the cultural and political conclusion of 1916. His school was not housed at Cullenswood by chance but appropriated significance from the belief that 'in Cullenswood House, Lecky, the famous historian, was born'.[2] Writing in the probable first edition of *An Macaomh*, and the only edition produced at Cullenswood, Pearse revealed his ambitions for his magazine and for the small school:

The Review will remain identified with our adventure at Sgoil Éanna as

---

1 Desmond Ryan, *Remembering Sion*, London 1934, p. 101
2 Milo McGarry 'Memories of Sgoil Éanna', *Capuchin Annual*, 1930, p. 35

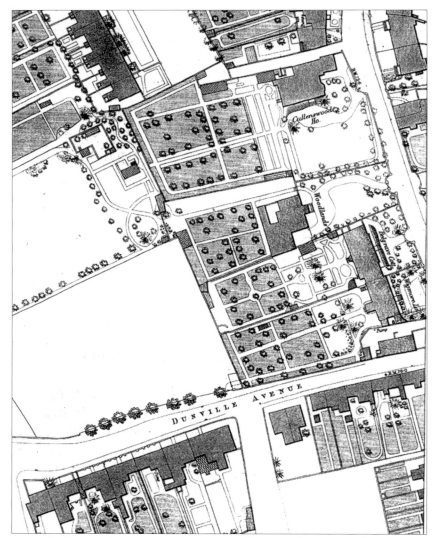

1888 Ordnance Survey map showing Cullenswood House and its gardens (top right), scale five inches to a mile.

long as the two endure, but I think it will become less and less of a School Magazine as time goes on. My hope is that it will come to be regarded as a rallying-point for the thought and aspirations of all those who would bring back again in Ireland that Heroic Age which reserved its highest honour for the hero with the most childlike heart.[3]

The school's ambition in the arts was revealed in the care given to describing the school's paintings, listing 'The Man that buried Raftery' by J. B. Yeats, a 'Mater Dolorosa' by William Pearse (copy of same in the Mortuary Chapel, St Andrew's, Westland Row, Dublin 2) and a watercolour view entitled 'In County Wicklow' by Patrick Tuohy.[4] In the spirit of the Arts and Crafts movement, Pearse also maintained that society had 'not yet that love for the beautiful which burned in the heart of the Middle Ages'.[5]

St Enda's was to become a true *Gesamtkunstwerke* environment, where all elements of the school's design and educational philosophy worked together to combine into a sum greater than the individual parts. Pearse also tried to ensure that significant people visited his school and that, in turn, his pupils visited significant places and people. A noted visitor was Roger Casement who spoke to the pupils of the 'Irish Revival'. Festivals and pageants were part of the curriculum at Cullenswood, and in 1910 Sir Henry Bellingham invited all the students down to the Castle Bellingham Feis to act once more the Cúchulainn pageant.[6]

Cullenswood House betrays its age in the 1888 Ordnance Survey map of the site in the manner in which it stands out from the otherwise Victorian suburban grain of the area. Unlike the other villas and terraced houses, it does not observe the orientation of the road, turning instead to face the sun and the distant vistas of the Dublin mountains. It had however, lost much of its substantial garden to neighbouring developments, but still possessed a large walled garden to the west of the house. The western elevation of the house acted as the garden front and not the true rear elevation, which gave directly onto a mews lane behind the house to the north. Steps led from the

3 *An Macaomh* 1st ed. (prob.) 1909 ed. by Patrick Pearse and published at St Enda's School
4 Ibid. pp. 8, 25, 29
5 Ibid. pp. 8, 25, 29
6 Milo McGarry, 'Memories of Sgoil Éanna', *Capuchin Annual*, 1930, p.38

Mícheál Mac Ruaidhrí, the gardening teacher, with his charges in the Cullenswood garden.

west elevation of the house down to the walled gardens.

The Pearse Museum has one photograph of the Cullenswood pupils hard at work with Mícheál Mac Ruaidhrí, the resident Irish-speaking gardener and teacher. In the background of the photograph the returns of suburban houses are clearly visible and it may have been taken looking southwards down one of the garden's gravelled pathways with the gable wall of the suburban villa Woodlands and the terraced houses of Dunville Avenue in the distance. A shed, perhaps for bicycles, lies beyond Mícheál Mac Ruaidhrí in the photograph and also appears on the 1888 map. Interestingly, not all of Mac Ruaidhrí's nine pupils are in the school uniform of kilt and crested jumper. The boy with the shears is wearing suspiciously unsuitable shoes for gardening although his neighbour, who seems to have received a dispensation to wear trousers and jacket, is wearing more practical wellies. A line of clipped topiary separates this productive garden from the lawns of the entrance area.

The school garden was a common garden typology in early 20th-century Europe, where self-sufficiency in wartime was of national importance. Expertise was relatively easy to come by as many families still cultivated food at home in their own gardens. The publication *Irish Gardening*, published frequent articles on 'The School Garden' by a Mr

Cullenswood House in the 1920s.

L. J. Humphrey, who was a 'special Instructor in School Gardening under the Department of Agriculture and Technical Instruction for Ireland'. He described the characteristics of a school garden in Ireland at this time:

> Although school gardens in Ireland are not so numerous as might be expected from the agricultural character of the country, there are a number of such gardens in connection with schools of various kinds. Nearly all of them are worked on the individual plot system, a plot being placed in charge of one or two pupils. The size of the gardens varies, but a garden of about a quarter of an acre is a most satisfactory size for a country school.[7]

Patrick Pearse had had the opportunity to visit and examine one of the most ambitious and beautiful Irish school gardens during his employment as a part-time lecturer (at university examination level) by Alexandra, a Protestant girls' college.[8] The school's patron at this time was Hermione, the third Duchess of Leinster, who had created a wonderful Arts and Crafts garden on her Carton estate in Kildare. As Alexandra College's principal mentor, it is unlikely that the Duchess

7 *Irish Gardening*, vol. 3, 1908, p.143
8 Ruth Dudley Edwards *The Triumph of Failure*, Dublin 1990, p.108

would not have advised the school about garden design, which was one of her great interests. Pearse had also acted as an examiner in Irish history for the Jesuit College for boys, Clongowes Wood,[9] in Co. Kildare, which is still set in extensive grounds leading down to the river Liffey.

Cullenswood garden consciously kept elements of its 19th-century ornamental walled garden layout, in its metamorphosis into a school garden. It seems likely that Pearse admired the recreational and aesthetic elements contained within these other school gardens and wished his school to observe and continue existing planting traditions. *Irish Gardening* devoted a large article to St Enda's in 1913, writing that 'no school in Ireland (or for that matter in England either) . . . approaches so near to the ideals of all true educationalists'.[10] Pearse's school garden became a model of its type.

As a location for his school Pearse began to believe that Cullenswood had disadvantages, and these arose primarily from its suburban location. Denis Gwynn, an ex-pupil, maintained that the school's aim of bilingual education was frustrated as it was 'necessary to do nearly all the teaching of other subjects, except for the very small children, in English'. This arose from the influence of the 'majority of day-boys who kept the school constantly under the influence of suburban surroundings, made it impossible to hope for any improvement in this respect'.

Denis Gwynn asserted in his article of 1923 that it 'was partly a realization of this permanent difficulty that led Pearse to remove from Dublin to the large grounds at Rathfarnham called "the Hermitage"'.[11] Pearse himself wrote a more heroic account of the reasons for the school's move in the 1910 edition of *An Macaomh*:

> I had convinced myself that the work I had planned to do for my pupils was impossible of accomplishment at Cullenswood. We were, so to speak, too much in the Suburban Groove. The city was too near; the hills too far. The house itself, beautiful and roomy though it was, was not large enough for our swelling numbers.

Cullenswood's playing field, the large field west of the walled

9 Ibid.
10 'St Enda's school gardens and pleasure grounds', *Irish Gardening*, VI, 1913, p. 26
11 Denis Gwynn, 'Patrick Pearse' in *The Dublin Review*, Jan–Mar 1923, p. 96

The view from Pearse's study at the Hermitage, Rathfarnham, looking over the overgrown walled garden. The Hell Fire Club is visible on the hillside in the distance.

gardens, was also a reason for the school's move. Although the boys had 'trained themselves there to be the cleverest hurlers in Dublin', Pearse found that it 'gave no scope for that spacious outdoor life, that intercourse with the wild things of the woods and the wastes (the only things in Ireland that know what freedom is)'.

Only in the more distant Rathfarnham could the boys enjoy 'that daily adventure face to face with elemental Life and Force, with its moral discipline, with its physical hardening, which ought to play so large a part in the education of a boy'. He reminded his readers that the school's ideal was the play-green of Eamhain, where the 'most gracious of all education systems had its finest expression'. He concluded with typical ambition that 'in a word, St Enda's had the highest aim in education of any school in Ireland: it must have the worthiest home'.[12]

The school's new setting was the Hermitage, a small suburban demesne of 50 acres located close to Rathfarnham Castle in southwest Dublin. Once successfully ensconced, Pearse began to develop the gardening programme he had started in the walled garden of Cullenswood. Nature study (*Dúil Eolas*), incorporating both 'practical

12 *An Macaomh*, 1910

gardening and Elementary Agriculture', formed 'an essential part of the work at St Enda's'. The boys' lessons did not 'take the form of a mere dry-as-dust teaching of the rudiments of zoology, botany & geology, but consists rather in an attempt to inspire a real interest in & love for beautiful things'.

The study began in the college garden and was continued during frequently organised outings to suitable spots within an easy radius of the college and 'each pupil who so desire[d]' was 'allotted a plot of ground' which he was 'at liberty to plan out and cultivate according to his own taste, but under skilled direction'.[13]

The skilled direction was again provided by Mícheál Mac Ruaidhrí, who had moved with Pearse from Cullenswood. He represented in person the hedge-school and warrior tradition Pearse wished to emulate. Desmond Ryan, an ex-pupil, remembered that Mícheál could 'dictate a history with only one pause for breath and chant a Rabelaisian or reverent Gaelic rann in his greenhouses as the mood takes him.'[14]

Another heartfelt description maintained that 'Mr Pearse's gardener' was 'a very vivid and racy personage' with 'a flavour of the wild earth and antique saga about him'. 'Nobody who takes grave and formal views of life would understand Mac Ruairi's place in Ireland.'[15]

Gardening was also helpful for teaching the economics of growing apples, which could pay for painting the classrooms. Kenneth Reddin, another ex-pupil, remembered being chastised for stealing apples, and of Pearse's intended use for the fruit:

'And then he [Pearse] remembered why he didn't want us to steal them. He hoped by the careful gathering, grading and packing to make enough money out of them to distemper three of the classrooms, including Matriculation, which was our own. The logic of this argument silenced us.'[16]

The Hermitage also possessed 'flower and vegetable gardens with their vineries, peach-houses and conservatories cover[ing] five acres . . . In the classrooms beautiful pictures, statuary, and plants replace[d] the charts and other paraphernalia of the ordinary schoolroom.'

13 National Library of Ireland (NLI), Ms. 5051, St Enda's prospectus 1911–12
14 Desmond Ryan *Remembering Sion*, London 1934, p. 115
15 W. P. Ryan *The Pope's Green Island*, London 1912, p. 297
16 Kenneth Reddin, 'A Man called Pearse', in *Studies, An Irish Quarterly Review*, Vol. XXXIV, June 1945, p. 244

The Central Walk at the Hermitage, planted with lavender.

Pearse wrote that by moving from Cullenswood, the school became 'situated in the healthiest, most beautiful and most romantic corner of south county Dublin.' In the outer reaches of Rathfarnham, it lay 'ringed by ancient legend and modern history' and these 'combine[d] to hallow the region in which the Three Rock Mountain, Tibradden, Kilmashogue, Ticknock, Montpelier and Glenasmole are landmarks.'

Located in the traditional villa setting of a hillside overlooking a town, its grounds 'command[ed] glorious prospects of the Dublin Hills . . . the Bay and the whole Dublin coastline.'[17] A photograph of the view from Pearse's study shows the distant eye catcher of the Hell Fire Club. It also reveals that the walled garden was substantially overgrown at the time of Pearse's move, and that exotic trees, such as the eucalyptus and the monkey puzzle were prominent in the area of the walled garden close to the house. Delighted with his new home, Pearse 'welcomed the 40 boys who gathered in twos and threes on the shaded path under the beeches and elms and sycamores near the fruit trees beyond the moss-green iron palings of the garden'.[18]

With the move, sporting activities certainly increased in prominence

17 NLI, Ms. 5051, prospectus 1911–12
18 Desmond Ryan *Remembering Sion,* London 1934, p. 94

[33]

The Hermitage's walled garden c.1913.

and possibilities, with Pearse listing 'hurling and football, a tennis court and handball' as school sports. A cycle track was also being laid down, it seems, and Pearse optimistically predicted that 'a swimming-bath will be provided'; it never was.[19]

The walled garden at the Hermitage was not dissimilar to the Cullenswood garden Pearse had left behind. It also lay southwest of the house, thereby ensuring that the house did not shadow it during the optimum periods of sunshine. Both gardens placed the more decorative and specimen plants in view of the windows of the house, and turnips, potatoes, onions and the more utilitarian produce was probably relegated to the most distant beds. These were further screened at the Hermitage by intervening orchard trees and planting which framed the interior paths. It is likely that the garden at Cullenswood also placed lavender, rosemary and other herbs on the verges of the principal cross-walks, providing a pleasant sensory experience for those taking their daily constitutional walk.

St Enda's library, now in the care of the Pearse Museum, contains books that probably contributed to the gardening programme. F. C. Hayes published *A Handy Book of Horticulture* in 1900, having been encouraged in his work 'by the knowledge that the new State Dept.

19 NLI, Ms. 5051, St Enda's prospectus 1911–12

of Agriculture and Technical Instruction for Ireland' had 'decided to promote the study of this Elementary Horticulture'.

It had been more than ten years since he had been invited by the Council of Alexandra College Dublin to undertake a lectureship in practical horticulture—at that time a new departure in education[20] at the college. As Pearse had also taught at Alexandra College it seems likely that the two men knew each other. Beeton's *Dictionary of Everyday Gardening*, shows signs of heavy use and somebody pasted-in lists of 'Brussels Sprouts and Winter Spinach & its substitutes'.[21]

The Hermitage had the space to house 'flower and vegetable gardens, fruit grounds, conservatories, greenhouses, vine and peach houses, propagating pits and all other conveniences and necessities of a well-equipped country mansion'.[22] The gardens were also managed as a profitable enterprise and fruit and vegetables not consumed by the school were sold. The following is an extract from a letter from Pearse to a Mr Wilson, dated June 1912, who was one of the school's many financial advisors. It demonstrates the appreciable role the sale of surplus produce played in the school's finances, as the rent for the house and demesne came to £300 per annum.

For 12 months June 30th 1911 to June 30th 1912

Income Received	£82 0s 0d from grazing rents
	£45 12s 7d from sales of vegetables
	£22 10s 10d from sales of livestock
Expenditure	£7 0s 0d garden expenses
	£5 0s 0d livestock bought[23]

A list of seeds contained in a 1931 account book suggests the vegetable varieties that the Pearse family probably planted at Cullenswood. Primarily a list of common vegetables, it also included '1 packet of hollyhocks'. It also listed the purchase of many utensils and fertilisers, which are not included here.

1 oz Turnip Rowan's early snowball

2 oz Turnip Orange Jelly

20 F. C. Hayes, *A Handy Book of Horticulture* London (John Murray), 1st edition 1900, reprint 1901, p vi
21 Beeton's *Dictionary of Everyday Gardening* London (Ward, Lock & Co.), 1883
22 'St. Enda's school gardens and pleasure grounds', *Irish Gardening*, VI, 1913, p. 27
23 NLI, Ms. 5051, Pearse Mss: Patrick Pearse to Mr Wilson, June 1912

1 packet Marrow Long White

3 lbs of Potatoes British Queen

No. 167 collection Antirrhinums

1 packet of Hollyhock

1 packet Thyme

1 packet Brussels Sprouts Rowans Exhibition

1 broccoli Rowan's early

Rowan's Queen of the ----[?]

April Queen

Rowans last of all

1 oz cabbage Ellams Early Enfield market

1 packet Savoy, Rowan's market garden

1 packet Leek Rowan's Giant

1 oz Tiepole[?] Giant Red Rocca

1 oz Parsnip Rowan's Champion

                         Hollow Browned

2 ozs Spinach   Prickly

1 oz Turnip   Rowan's Silver skinned

Total: £0 17s 4d[24]

The Pearse family did retain a connection with Cullenswood after the events of 1916. The school accounts for 1914–50 contain a poignant 'Army Services Form of Advice, Draft and Receipt to the amount of £8 6s 11d' sent to Pearse's mother on 17 August 1917 by 'the Cashier's Office of the Irish Command'. She inscribed the draft, which she never cashed:

> Received the above sum . . . paid to me as an 'Act of Grace' in full discharge of all claims arising out of loss alleged to have been suffered by me while in Military Custody on account of the recent rebellion.[25]

The accounts reveal that Mrs Pearse paid the 'rent for Cullenswood' on 19 May 1919 to Hugh G. Levingstone.[26]

What was lost when Scoil Éanna moved to Rathfarnham? Strangely

24 NLI, Ms. 21090, f.2: Bill for seeds and plants, 4 March 1913: 'from M. Rowan & son, Seed Bulb & Plant Merchants est. 1889, 51 & 51 Capel St'
25 NLI, Pearse Mss, Ms. 21090, f.1: 'Form of Advice, Draft and Receipt to the amount of £8,6,11
26 NLI, Pearse Mss, Ms. 21090, Accounts 1914–50

enough, and despite the new location's 'scope for outdoor life', probably some of the gardening education. Scoil Éanna's *Clár na hOibre* 1915–16 reveals that the fifth and final year in the Hermitage did not do *Dúil Eolas* (nature study), unlike in Cullenswood, where both the fifth and sixth years took the subject. All the fourth years took four and a half hours of *Dúil Eolas* per week and one timetable suggests that the third years took one and a half hours of *Obair láimhe* (manual work) with Mícheál Mac Ruaidhrí. However, alternative timetables are pencilled over the remaining timetables in the National Library of Ireland and it may have been removed from the curriculum.[27]

With the school's move to Rathfarnham, the pedagogical programme did acquire a more masculine and secondary focus. The emphasis on 'manual work', so suggestive of Maria Montessori's pedagogical theory, seems to have been modified for the older cohort of pupils. Sequestered in the more distant landscape of Rathfarnham, and away from the interfering influence of home life, Pearse could concentrate on propagating revolution. It is also probable that Pearse's move from Cullenswood to Rathfarnham contributed to the school's eventual closure, as heroic and revolutionary landscape is rarely compatible with the day-to-day prosaic requirements of children's education and care.

The humdrum environment of suburbia could also have reduced the notoriety and attention the school received in the aftermath of Easter 1916, which contributed to its eventual demise. The cohort of day pupils at Cullenswood ensured that Pearse and his school had to engage with the surrounding society and the attendant levels of parental (and female) supervision. These restraints were consciously removed in the demesne villa landscape of the Hermitage, a Utopian pedagogical landscape both screened and defined by the smooth ribbon of demesne wall.[28] Pearse's landscape design became both revolutionary and unsustainable in Rathfarnham. Cullenswood, with the return of Lios na nÓg to the refurbished house, can be planted again, 'in the suburban groove'.

27 NLI, Ms. 21288, Scoil Éanna: Clár na hOibre, 1915–16
28 For a complete discussion of the evolution of the landscape of St Enda's, Rathfarnham, see: Finola O'Kane, 'Nurturing a Revolution: Patrick Pearse's School Garden at St Enda's', *Garden History, Journal of the Garden History Society*, vol 28: no. 1, Summer 2000, pp. 73–88

A Cullenswood childhood: Growing up in the big house in the 1950s

Deirdre Donnelly

The ten years that our family lived in Cullenswood House provided my sisters and me with a memorable childhood. Even though, at the end of that decade, we only moved as far away as Beechwood Avenue, the wrench was considerable. In leaving Cullenswood, we left behind a childhood lived in leafy orchards, wide lawns and large graceful rooms. We also left behind a community of people who had, over the years, become as familiar to us as our own family. A great nostalgia still remains with us for our early years in Cullenswood House.

Cullenswood in the 1950s had gateposts topped by stone lions and black iron gates opening onto a gravel driveway which was dominated by two large beech trees. There was a small gate-lodge with a little garden to one side of the house, a wide lawn to the front and an orchard at the end of the house, separated from the rest of the garden by a hedge and black iron railings. At the back of the house there were disused outhouses. In the adjacent house (now the Canadian Embassy) in Oakley Road lived the Corcorans, a medical family, while on the other side of Cullenswood, the next-door neighbour was Senator Brady.

Although somewhat overgrown, the orchard still had peaches, pears, gooseberries etc., alongside the apple trees, of such good quality that the surplus often supplied Morton's, the local greengrocer's in Dunville Avenue. The orchard extended as far as Beechwood Park, encompassing the land on which Scoil Bhríde now stands. There were lilac trees and a Viburnum snowball-tree in the orchard, with blossoms which we always begged for, to bring to school for the May altars. My sisters, Pauline and Terry, and I spent much of our time in the school holidays playing in the orchard, where hens clucked and pecked about. The hens belonged to the Cooling family who lived

Mrs Pearse and her daughter Margaret—later the Donnellys' landlady—on the steps of Cullenswood House.

there in a small cottage. We would walk down the leafy orchard paths or climb the trees, balancing precariously on summer sandals.

Sometimes we re-enacted the cowboys and Indians films we had seen at the Saturday matinée in the Sandford cinema in Ranelagh with titles like *Fort Massacre* or *Black Horse Canyon*, fashioning bows and arrows from thin branches, bending the bow into a curve while we stretched twine taut between the two ends. We climbed, ran, argued, hid and played for hours in the orchard. When we had exhausted its possibilities, we would go back out through the small black iron orchard gate, dodging the wasps around the fuchsia bush, emerging onto the gravel driveway in front of the house.

We took turns on the swing that our father had erected for us in the big sycamore tree across the lawn and swung up high enough to see over the wall into Corcorans' garden next door. My sister Terry maintains that there was a maze in their garden, but being the smallest, I wasn't able to swing high enough to see it. There must have been a pond there too, because at the base of the front wall in Cullenswood, in amongst the damp overgrown ivy, little escapee frogs occasionally hopped about. We tried to catch them in shoeboxes, but they always leaped to freedom.

Fledglings fell now and then from nests in the old beech trees in the driveway. We would do our best to keep them alive but they never survived our ministrations. At the far end of the lawn was what we called the 'fort'. This was a steep mound of earth which you had to run up quickly before you lost momentum. The horizontal roots of a large tree provided footholds, and you steadied yourself at the top by grabbing the lower-hanging branches for balance. At the top, elderberry bushes grew wild, and ruined brickwork walls suggested that at one time there must have been a small building there of some sort. From the fort we would survey the comings and goings of the house. Over at the clothesline in a secluded corner of the garden, our mother would hang out the clothes after a morning's strenuous washing indoors at the kitchen sink. Items such as Irish linen or good damask tablecloths, however, were sent to the Swastika Laundry and were delivered back by van a few days later, neatly packaged with brown paper and string.

The mothers in Cullenswood often joined forces to brush down the hallway and stairs. Damp tea-leaves would be sprinkled over the stairs to trap dust, and the residue would be swept away with dustpan and brush, leaving the hall and stairs clean. Then, on hands and knees, they would apply the floor polish. Often we were employed to skate up and down on polishing-cloths to shine the floor. Mr Cooling might pass by on his way down to Ranelagh. His cottage, unlike the main house, was not connected to the electricity supply, so from time to time he

The Donnelly family, who lived in Cullenswood House in the 1950s.

would take the 'wet battery' of the radio down to the electrical shop in Ranelagh in order to get it recharged. In the shop, the battery would be re-filled and this would power the radio for another few weeks.

Mr Holden, Miss Margaret Pearse's agent for collecting the rent, called from time to time, marking up the payments in books kept on a ledge inside the front door. The bread-man would park his van outside the gates and come up the steps of Cullenswood to deliver loaves and turnovers wrapped in brown tissue paper. Often he would give us the bread to bring up to our mother. By the time she got it, there was every possibility that a large crater had appeared in the bread, hidden under the brown tissue paper, where we hadn't been able to resist picking pieces out of the fresh loaf.

At weekends, the men of the house would take turns tidying the garden, hoeing weeds from the driveway, cutting hedges or mowing the lawn. On the driveway, our father taught us to ride a bicycle when we were old enough. He had bought two second-hand black Raleigh 'High Nelly' bicycles from the Misses Ferguson—two ladies who lived further down Oakley Road at the end of the terrace. He spent many weekends patiently holding us upright until the moment when we wobbled away, pedalling furiously on our first solo flight around the garden. If the bicycle got a puncture, he would turn it upside down to repair it, prising off the tyre with the handle of a spoon and placing the inner tube in a white enamel basin of water. The little telltale bubbles from the tube would reveal the puncture and a rubber patch was stuck on with foul-smelling glue. The tyre was then replaced and the wheel pumped up. Usually a little audience of interested children would gather around to watch this tricky procedure.

Winters in Cullenswood could be severe. My sister Pauline recalls: 'In bad weather, the two large beech trees in the driveway swayed and groaned and threw shadows against the house while the rain lashed the windowpanes. There were no lights to guide you in the driveway, and once you got to the front door, you had to wait in the darkness for someone to come down and open the door. A white figure was said to have appeared from time to time in one of the rooms off the hall, asking for prayers. Knowing this made for a few anxious moments until you scurried up the stairs to safety.'

Like many houses in the 1950s, Cullenswood House had no central heating. Getting up on a cold winter's morning involved mentally steeling yourself for the unavoidable moment when you had to plunge from the warmth of the blankets onto the ice-cold lino of the bedroom floor. Our mother would warm our clothes in front of a little gas fire and there, shivering, we would get dressed. When snow fell we would run around to Beechwood Park, where children would take turns sliding on a long stretch of icy path. With no cars there to disturb us, this was an ideal place to enjoy the snow. When our woollen mittens got wet from playing snowballs and our fingers began to sting with icy pain, we would run back home where our mother would give us dry woolly socks to put on our hands, while she hung the wet mittens on the fireguard to dry. We would dash back out, not wanting to miss a minute of the snow. On one such winter morning, outside the gate of Cullenswood House, the horse attached to the milkman's dray slipped on the ice and collapsed onto the road. I can still remember the crash as the horse hit the ground, pulling the dray and all the glass milk bottles over. Shattered glass and milk covered the ground, as the milkman struggled to un-strap the horse from the dray and get it to its feet.

This happened almost outside the gate-lodge where Miss de Cadiz lived. To my child's eye Miss de Cadiz seemed to be very old and due to the large number of cats she kept, her little garden with its trellis fence always had a vague whiff of tomcat. One of her twelve cats was named Winston Churchill. In later times I read that Rosalind de Cadiz and her sister had, as young women, been Voluntary Aid Detachment (VAD) nurses serving in the First World War. Miss de Cadiz had sustained injuries in the course of her duties and had been awarded a medal for her contribution to the war effort. Her name, along with that of her sister, appears on the Roll of Honour in the Mariners' Church, Dún Laoghaire. Her father, Captain de Cadiz, occasionally visited her in Cullenswood and stopped by for a chat with our parents upstairs.

On 12 October 2009, a letter appeared in *The Irish Times* requesting information on Leila and Rosalind de Cadiz, which opened the fascinating story of the sisters' earlier lives. They were both active in the Irish Women's Franchise League in Dublin and went to London in 1911 to continue their militancy under Sylvia Pankhurst, for which they spent time in Holloway Prison. Leila went on hunger strike and was force-fed. They continued their work in Dublin and were incarcerated in Mountjoy with Hanna Sheehy-Skeffington in 1912.

Our family had originally lived in the ground floor flat at the rear of the house which overlooked the orchard, but when the Tyrell family vacated the upstairs front flat, we moved up there instead, as the rooms afforded lovely views of the lawn and the beech trees. In former times Richard Mulcahy, Chief of Staff of the IRA, had lived in this upstairs flat with his family. During the War of Independence, the house had been raided by the English military forces on many occasions. Once, they had fired bullets through the front door, narrowly missing Mrs Mulcahy's baby.

Another raid led to 'the discovery of the IRA Headquarters at Cullenswood House . . . where rolls and addresses of 3,000 Dublin IRA Brigade members were found'.[1] In later years I came across old newspaper reports describing the worst raid on Cullenswood House on 30 January 1921, when 'all but Mrs Pearse had left the house in December owing to repeated raids'.[2] *The Irish Times* reported that

1 William Sheehan *Fighting for Dublin: The British Battle for Dublin 1919–1921* (The Collins Press, Cork 2007) p. 11
2 *New York Times* 31 January 1921: report from a Belfast correspondent: PEARSE HOUSE WRECKED

CULLENSWOOD HOUSE.

WHAT THE MILITARY FOUND.

SECRET DOORS AND DUMMY WALLS.

According to official statements the action of the military in St. Enda's College, Dublin, on Sunday, was not in the nature of a reprisal on account of the ambushing of the military at Terenure on the previous day. The military, it appears, merely went to the college to investigate some recent suspicious and unnecessary structural alterations to the building, and these were removed. No unnecessary damage was done.

A further report states that the entry of soldiers into the house was due to the fact that a recent search disclosed several suspicious and apparently unnecessary structural alterations that had been recently made, the details for the building of which and the estimate were in the handwriting of leading rebels. It was, therefore, decided to ascertain the reason for the alterations.

Minute investigations resulted in the discovery that the changes were in the nature of false walls and false doors, and there was a false wardrobe, with a secret spring, which opened into a chamber that appeared to be used as an office. In one of the rooms secret doors and secret cupboards were found. There were nine exit doors giving access to adjacent fields.

During the investigations a revolver and some ammunition were found in one of the dummy walls. Previous raids showed that the premises had been used to carry out the object of an illegal association. There was nobody on the premises yesterday, but in a room a supper had been laid, apparently for people on the previous night.

The Irish Times *1 February 1921, reporting the British military's account of their raid on Cullenswood House.*

Cullenswood House

was completely wrecked by parties of men who arrived at the scene in motor lorries and brought with them crowbars, picks, saws and other implements. The work of destruction was carried on for several hours and was executed in a most thorough fashion, the building and out-offices being left in ruins. The conservatories were razed to the ground, the slated roof of the house demolished, all the windows and doors smashed and the furniture broken up.[3]

The *Freeman's Journal* showed photographs of an armoured car patrolling Oakley Road, the armed soldiers squatting on the front wall guarding the gates, and their colleagues on the roof of Cullenswood hacking at the slates with pickaxes.[4] The *Freeman's Journal* regretted the destruction of the large front room on the ground floor which had been the library of the father of renowned historian William Edward Hartpole Lecky.[5] The raid lasted several hours. However, the following day the military authorities alleged that they had discovered 'false walls and false doors and there was a false wardrobe with a secret spring which opened into a chamber that appeared to be used as an office'. There were also, they said, 'nine exit doors giving access to adjacent fields' and 'a revolver and some ammunition had been found in one of the dummy walls'.[6]

These allegations may have been propaganda by the authorities to justify their actions in all but demolishing the house. However, it was well known in nationalist circles that Michael Collins used Cullenswood House as one of his offices and IRA headquarters, and so it is quite possible that there was truth in the allegations, and that Collins would have had his exit well prepared, in the event of just such a raid. Mrs Pearse must have been a resilient woman indeed to have withstood alone this violent attack on her house. Fortunately, neighbours and friends came to her assistance. The house was later restored and was to see more peaceful days in times to come.

3 *The Irish Times* Monday 31 January 1921: CULLENSWOOD HOUSE PARTIALLY WRECKED, p. 5
4 *Freeman's Journal* Tuesday 1 February 1921, p. 3
5 Ibid. HISTORIC HOUSE WRECKED. CROWN FORCES DESTRUCTION AT CULLENSWOOD HOUSE. OFFICIAL REPORT MRS. PEARSE AND THE MYSTERIOUS DISCOVERIES, p. 4
6 *The Irish Times*, Tuesday 1 February 1921: CULLENSWOOD HOUSE: WHAT THE MILITARY FOUND. SECRET DOORS AND DUMMY WALLS, p.5

*The three Donnelly girls, Terry, Deirdre
and Pauline in front of the house.*

Thirty years later when we lived there, Cullenswood showed none of
the damage done to it by the 'troubles' of the 1920s and had resumed
its former air of mellow propriety. Apart from the occasional puffing
of a steam train pulling out of the station on Beechwood Road and
continuing its journey towards the bridge near the end of Oakley Road,
nothing much disturbed the mornings except perhaps a street violinist
playing waltzes further down the road, the milkman's horse clopping
slowly between houses, knowing from experience which house to stop
at, or a black Morris Minor making its way towards Dunville Avenue.

Along with the Cooling family in the orchard cottage and Miss
de Cadiz in the gate-lodge, the residents of Cullenswood who came
and went during our time there were, to the best of my recollection,
the Tyrells, the Joyces, the O'Dwyers, Mrs McChesney, her daughter
Magdalen, her sister Miss Feeley, the Holloweds, the Nugents and our
family, the Donnellys. The Joyce family lived in the three rooms off the
hall—one on the right, overlooking the driveway and Oakley Road,
and two interconnecting rooms on the left, the furthest of which had
a French window overlooking the orchard. Pauline recalls: 'They also
had a room downstairs, a big kitchen and a scullery with a big stone

sink. There was also a door into that big area where I suppose Michael Collins was hidden—like a storage cellar—and then an area with a little window that overlooked the Coolings' house, and a bathroom with a loo on a plinth like a throne.'

The O'Dwyer family lived upstairs in the flat next to ours. Both Mrs O'Dwyer and her daughter Olwen were excellent pianists. Mrs O'Dwyer often invited me—all of four years old—to sit down by the fire while she played the piano and sang wartime songs such as 'Run, rabbit, run' or 'How much is that doggie in the window?' Mrs McChesney, her daughter Magdalen and her sister Miss Feeley lived on the ground floor, through the archway at the end of the stairs. The Hollowed family, originally from Ballyboden in Rathfarnham, took over our former flat on the ground floor when we moved upstairs, and when Mrs Hollowed's sister, Mrs Nugent and her new husband moved into what had been Mrs McChesney's flat, their wedding celebrations were held in Cullenswood House.

The tenants of the house operated in many ways as a community. There were good-humoured evenings when the adults played card games like Whist or Twenty-Five together around a table, with the hostess dispensing tea and sandwiches. The Holloweds invited us down to celebrate Hallowe'en with their daughter Marian, named after the Marian Year of 1954. Dressed in whatever old clothes we could borrow and wearing what our father called a 'vizard' (mask) made of cardboard, bought for us in Woolworths, we were entertained by the Holloweds with fruit, nuts, barmbrack and Hallowe'en games. Hands behind backs, we would try to bite a swinging apple on a string or plunge our faces into a basin of water to retrieve an apple or a thrupenny bit. Later on there were ghost stories by the fire.

The Joyces, in the front ground-floor flat, were equally welcoming. Pauline and Terry, who, together with Miriam Joyce, took piano lessons from Miss Quinn in Moyne Road, were allowed to practise the piano in the Joyces' sittingroom. Miriam's older sister, Helen—later to become a successful model and to marry radio and television presenter Terry Wogan—would make us glamorous by painting our nails with crimson nail varnish.

On rainy days we would sometimes play in the stone-floored basement, looking out now and then at the rain dripping on the bay and laurel bushes on either side of the front steps. Occasionally in summer, a birthday party was held on the lawn. Tables were brought out to the garden and the mothers handed round cake and glasses of red lemonade while we played on the lawn in our best starched summer frocks and patent-leather shoes.

In later years, another family, the Scarletts, came to live in Cullenswood House. Mr Scarlett was related to the Pearse family and was, I believe, Margaret Pearse's godson. He attended the military funeral of our grandfather, a GPO veteran, in 1958. For some years prior to 1916, my grandfather Patrick Donnelly, had lived and worked in St Enda's in Rathfarnham as a gardener alongside Micheál Mac Ruairí. Grandfather fought as a Volunteer in the GPO, was interned in Frongoch and in the ensuing years fought in the IRA right up to the end of the civil war. After his years of fighting, he became chief greenkeeper in the Grange Golf Club in Rathfarnham and lived on into his eighties. Our father often brought us to visit him in his cottage in rural Whitechurch in Rathfarnham. Grandfather would never send us home without a few bundles of newspaper in which he had carefully packed polyanthus, phlox, wallflowers or whatever else he had a surplus of, with earth and roots still attached, to be transplanted into the Cullenswood rockery and flowerbeds. Prior to that, when food-rationing was in force during the Emergency, the flowerbeds had been put to use growing vegetables, but since that was no longer necessary they could be replanted again with flowers.

Terry remembers occasions when, on our journey on the single-decker 47 bus to our grandfather's, we would be accompanied by Miss Pearse on her way into town, who would chat to our father whom she had known as a youngster when he lived in the gardener's cottage in St Enda's.

The Emergency had only ended a few short years before we came to live in Cullenswood House, so it is not surprising that, during our explorations of the attic, reached by opening a small door on the upper landing and going up a narrow flight of wooden stairs, we children found gas masks and ration books, discarded a few years earlier when the Emergency had ended. Terry recalls finding a large pile of children's books and comics there, among which were ones recounting the adventures of Joan 'Worralls' Worralson, British aviatrix and female equivalent of fictional war-hero Biggles. We never found out what little girl living in Cullenswood in the 1940s had read these stories in bed at night, avidly following the adventures of Worralls, pigtailed heroine of the skies.

Once, in 1957, the movies came to Ranelagh in the form of a film called *Rooney*. We heard that some of the filming was to be done just beside what was called the 'Black Church' (Church of the Holy Trinity) on Belgrave Road, and after much pleading, we persuaded our mother to bring us to watch a night-time scene being shot. The stars, Noel Purcell, Jack McGowran and John Gregson, in a horse and trap, were required to call a dog down from the doorway of the house. The dog was to run quickly down the steps, jump into the trap and the actors and dog would drive away. However, the dog had other ideas and it needed a lot of biscuits to persuade him to jump up into the trap. In the end, however, he got it right and as it was getting quite late we were ushered home to bed, triumphantly clutching our autograph books whose coloured pages had been signed by the actors.

Sometimes, at the weekends, after the grass had been mown and rolled with the heavy granite roller, a tennis court would be marked out on the lawn with white lime. Later, when the lime was dry, the old tennis net would be stretched across the lawn. The Elvery's tennis racquets would be unscrewed from their wooden frames, used to stop the racquet warping, and a game would begin. Our father and the other men would often dress for the occasion in white tennis trousers and white polo-shirts. That quintessential summer sound of racquet whacking tennis ball still brings to mind those games on the lawn in Cullenswood, accompanied by much laughter and banter. We children would play too, getting lots of advice from the adults.

The afternoon would drift pleasantly into evening and the mothers would sit on the steps, keeping an eye on us as we flitted about like moths, eking out the last glimmer of playtime before bed. 'In the long dusky evenings the bats swooped from the big sycamore tree in the middle of the garden and we were always warned about how they might get entangled in our hair,' Pauline remembers.

One night in 1957, we all stood in the gravel driveway and craned our necks heavenward to see the Russian Sputnik as it moved across the night sky. For long minutes we scanned the sky until suddenly our father said 'There it is!' and pointed to a particular star. Following the direction of his finger, we peeled our eyes until at last we saw it: across the heavens filled with static stars, one began to cut a path through the rest, traversing the night sky. The space age had begun. Finally, when it was no longer visible, our mother called us in to bed and we headed reluctantly indoors.

In the hallway, around the half-moon fanlight above the door, old Gaelic lettering remained from the St Enda's days, displaying the words of the boy Cúchulainn: 'It is a wonderful thing even if I am but one day and one night in the world, provided my fame and deeds live after me.' We climbed the stairs to bed. Tomorrow we would call for Margaret Finn, our friend in Dunville Avenue, or Tom Doyle, the boy across the road, and go up to Mrs Mooney's sweetshop to buy Honey-Bees and lucky-bags. Tucked up in bed in the old house which had seen children of many generations come and go, we couldn't possibly understand just how fortunate we were to spend a unique childhood in Cullenswood House, and to experience, to the full, the 'congenial environment and loving watchfulness' which Pearse, the visionary educationalist, considered essential to the development of the child.

Pauline Donnelly on the steps of Cullenwood House.

Feeding and freeing the imagination:
Scoil Bhríde

Éilis Ní Dhuibhne

A picture or carving or statue, looked at with understanding, teaches a lesson that is not easily forgotten. At the same time, the reverent and thorough study of a great work of art kindles the imagination to the perception and appreciation of beauty . . . For junior classes, the principal aim will be to link the various parts of the picture, emphasising the dormant meaning.[1]

Thus writes Louise Gavan Duffy, founder of Scoil Bhríde, in one of the few writings she had published during her long and productive life. A passion for art was one of her defining characteristics, although not the one which would first spring to mind in association with this patriot, educationalist, and cultural nationalist. The little booklet from which the above citation is drawn—*School Studies in the Appreciation of Art*— reveals plenty about its author, however. The most unusual aspect of the booklet is that it is tri-lingual, written in Irish, English and French, reflecting Louise Gavan Duffy's three languages. These were the three languages taught in Scoil Bhríde, the first all-Irish school since the end of the Penal Days, according to one of its eminent past pupils and most committed supporters, Donn Piatt.[2]

The elegantly written text reveals a deep knowledge and love of European painting, mixed with a deep religious fervour and a zeal for teaching. One could say that this little booklet, a pamphlet preserved in the National Library of Ireland, symbolises all that was crucial about Scoil Bhríde: its focus on language and religion, its ambitious syllabus. Absent, though, from this history of European art is the

1 *School Studies in the Appreciation of Art* by Lúise Ghabhánach Ní Dhubthaigh and Eilís Ní Eachanaich. Dublin, University College Dublin, 1932
2 Donn Piatt, 'Gearrchúntas ar Stair Scoil Bhríde' in *Lúise Ghabhánach Ní Dhufaigh agus Scoil Bhríde*, eag. Máiréad Ní Ghacháin, Baile Átha Cliath, 1993

Seventh class, Scoil Bhríde 1934.

patriotism which was the single key ingredient in the school ethos, at its foundation in 1917 and for very long afterwards. This patriotism was still very much alive when I attended the school, from 1959 to 1966. But what the booklet reveals is that it was a patriotism which was broad, not narrow. Scoil Bhríde was primarily devoted to Gaeilge and Ireland. But it did not forget its place in Europe, its connection to France, at a time when few primary schools could have been so international.

I suspect that art appreciation was part of the syllabus in the early days, and Louise Gavan Duffy emerges as a sort of Sister Wendy from the pages of *School Studies in the Appreciation of Art*. The subject probably depended on her, however, and was not taught at all when I was a student there in the 1960s. Indeed, there were no art classes of any kind, perhaps reflecting the general syllabus of the era. The paintings, however, which I guess Louise Gavan Duffy used, still hung on the walls of the school. Reproductions of 'The Adoration of the Lamb' by the Brothers Van Eyck, various 'Adorations of the Magi', Botticelli's 'Angelus'.

It is very important for children to see beautiful things and to be schooled in pleasant, attractive surroundings. The Scoil Bhríde I

Eighth class, Scoil Bhríde 1934.

attended was housed in 19 Earlsfort Terrace, a Georgian house which had once been charming but which had deteriorated to a state of near dereliction by the 1960s. But it contained some touches of beauty.

On its damp and peeling walls hung reproductions of some great masterpieces, placed there, no doubt, by Louise Gavan Duffy. On the first of May, in a little May Day celebration which I have not come across in other schools, all these paintings were taken down and girls—honoured girls, who were also not fidgety—stood around the playground, backs to the crumbling yellow brick wall with pink valerian and buddleia sprouting out of its crevices, holding the pictures, while the rest of the school processed around, dressed in their summer frocks or communion dresses, carrying bouquets and singing hymns.

The sun shone on the sheltered yard, filled with the smell of flowers and the children's voices, and the paintings were displayed as in an open air gallery. This was one of the loveliest things that happened in Scoil Bhríde.

By then, the 1960s, Louise Gavan Duffy was a very old woman. Tall, stooped, dressed in long black clothes and a pudding bowl hat, the uniform of all old women in those days, she would visit the school regularly, perhaps once a month, and so we knew her to see. Our foundress. The other national schools did not have visiting foundresses who looked like messengers from another age. In Scoil Bhríde, we were aware that we were special. And we were acutely aware of our connection to the past, although we were not always knowledgeable as to its precise details.

They are the following. Louise Gavan Duffy was born in Nice, in 1887. Her father was Sir Charles Gavan Duffy, founder of the *Nation*, who had been a leader in the Young Ireland rebellion of 1848. Her mother was Louise Hall, her father's third wife. They married in 1862, had four children, and she died in 1889, pre-deceasing him by many years although she was about forty years his junior.

Louise Gavan Duffy was brought up in Nice, speaking French and English. According to her own account, she did not know the Irish language even existed at all until she was fifteen. The story is that she came across a reference to *A Grammar of the Irish Language* in a bookseller's catalogue, and asked her father what this language was. Thereupon she vowed to learn it—which she did, when she came to Ireland in 1907, to attend University College Dublin (UCD). She took classes, like so many at the time, in Conradh na Gaeilge and became proficient.

Although her family knew no Irish, she was intensely aware of Irish history. '*Tógadh sinn i dtraidisiún 1848,*' she said, in an interview given in the early 1960s.[3] ('We were brought up in the tradition of 1848'— that is, the tradition of the Young Irelanders). The Gavan Duffys' nationalist connections were sturdy. The Fenian John O'Leary was best man at her parents' wedding. Douglas Hyde was a frequent enough visitor to the villa in Nice, where he told stories to the children.

In Conradh na Gaeilge Louise Gavan Duffy met Patrick Pearse. He came in to her class as an examiner, and she was impressed by what we could call his charisma, although she said you could not say he was handsome. (She was striking looking herself, with a head of long red hair, much commented upon by those who knew her in her youth.)

The history of Scoil Bhríde is closely linked with that of Scoil Éanna and Scoil Íde (always pronounced 'Íte' at that time, according to Donn Piatt). Pearse opened Scoil Éanna in Cullenswood House, where Lios na nÓg is now, in 1908. Scoil Éanna was a school for boys,

3 Donn Piatt, op. cit. p. 1

ST. ITA'S SCHOOL,

Cullenswood House,

(Oakley Road), Rathmines,

Dublin.

A Boarding and Day School for Catholic Girls
(in association with ST. ENDA'S SCHOOL, Rathfarnham).

DIRECTOR	P. H. Pearse, B.A., Barrister-at-Law (Head Master of ST. ENDA'S SCHOOL).
HOUSE MISTRESS	Mrs. Bloomer.
ASSISTANT RESIDENT MISTRESS	Miss Mary Cotter, B.A. (Diplomée with Distinctions in Teaching, University of Cambridge; Special Prizewinner R.U.I. Studentship in Celtic).
ASSISTANT MISTRESSES	Miss Lena Butler, M.A. (Honours Diplomée in Teaching, R.U.I.). Miss M. C. Maguire, B.A. Miss Browner.
SPECIAL SUBJECTS.	
MUSIC (Irish Harp)	Miss C. Hayden.
" (Violin)	Miss Emily Keady.
" (Piano and Vocal)	Mrs. Bloomer (Ex-Sch. and Gold Medallist, R.I.A.M).
ART	William Pearse.
DRILL AND GYMNASIUM	William Carroll (Amateur International Gymnastic Champion).

St Ita's staff, from a prospectus.

which placed special emphasis on teaching Irish, but was not, in fact, an all-Irish school. In 1910, Scoil Éanna moved to new premises at the Hermitage in Rathfarnham, and Pearse opened a school for girls, Scoil Íde, in Cullenswood House. He employed Louise Gavan Duffy as a teacher, although he himself was headmaster of the school—*in absentia*. He came in once a fortnight to give a history lesson to the girls. '*Tá mé cinnte nár chuala aon dream cailíní roimhe sin ná ó shin, ceachtanna staire chomh bríomhar, suimiúil leo sin,*' Louise Gavan Duffy remembered. ('I am sure that no group of girls has before or since had such lively, interesting history lessons.')

Scoil Íde closed down in 1912, probably owing to financial difficulties. Louise Gavan Duffy then attended Dominican College, Eccles Street to take the Cambridge Teacher's Diploma, and remained in that institution as an assistant teacher until 1917, when she, and her friend Áine Nic Aodha, founded Scoil Bhríde. In the interim she participated in the 1916 Rising. Although opposed to the rebellion, the reason being the pragmatic one that she believed it was doomed to failure, she went to the GPO on Easter Monday evening and helped out in the kitchen for the week, cooking and washing up. Her attitude to the Rising seems peculiar in its ambivalence, but one can recall that such ambivalence was shared by, say, W. B. Yeats, and perhaps was not uncommon among thoughtful people.

On 5 September 1917, Scoil Bhríde opened in 70, St Stephen's Green. There were five teachers on the staff, and 12 pupils on the first day. By the end of the year, 100 had enrolled. The school catered for girls to the age of 16, and so was a secondary as well as a primary school. It was successful enough, but it suffered from financial difficulties. Numbers fell during and after the Civil War. It is not easy to get an honest reason for this, even so long after the event. By certain accounts, the methods of the school were too modern for many. But a more likely explanation of falling numbers after 1921 is that Louise Gavan Duffy's pro-Treaty stance did not endear her or her school to many of the parents.

Like so much in Ireland, the story of Scoil Bhríde is one of networks, alliances and connections. Conveniently and, indeed, crucially for the future of the school, its co-founder Áine Nic Aodha married Earnán de Blaghad. In 1926, when he was Minister for Finance, he rescued Scoil Bhríde from potential closure by making it a National School—which meant that the Department of Education paid the teachers' salaries while the school tried to meet all other expenses. The school had already changed premises, and from 1922 until 1931, was based on Pembroke Road. One of the pupils in Pembroke Road, and then on the Terrace, was Maeve Brennan, from Ranelagh, who later became a short story writer of great note. Other well-known past pupils, of a later vintage, include singer Liam Ó Maonlaí, the poet Biddy Jenkinson and cultural entrepreneur, Laura Magahy. No doubt there are many others.

Apart from belonging to a network of Irish speakers and patriots who had influence in government and in other circles, Scoil Bhríde had what must have been an unusual link for a national school, with UCD. This seems to have come about thanks to the involvement of Louise Gavan Duffy with the Education Department in the university. She taught some courses in UCD. One result of the contact was that UCD used Scoil Bhríde as a school in which students taking the Higher Diploma in Education—the H. Dip—could do their teaching practice. This was mutually advantageous. The students had a school close at hand in which to practice, and Scoil Bhríde benefited from teaching by young, university-educated and usually extremely idealistic and committed trainee teachers.

In my day, these teachers came in a few times a week, often to teach French. It was thanks to the UCD link that we were introduced to *La Vie de Madame Souris* in third class, I think, and continued to have French lessons until sixth (mostly using *La Vie de Madame Souris*, though eventually we graduated to the Folens *French Course for Irish Secondary Schools* and were entertained by that exciting bunch of people, La famille Latour—Jean, Louise, Maman and Papa. There was a baby and perhaps a poodle, too.

We also had some excellent teachers of English, young nuns who came over from UCD. Under the tutelage of a particular nun whose name I unforgiveably forget, we wrote poems, short stories, and even a play, which we performed in 1965 on the wonderful stage in the hall in the new school on Oakley Road, Ranelagh. These nuns were the only religious teachers I met as a child, and they were creative and inspirational. They loved children, English, and teaching, and did not seem especially interested in religion, but this was perhaps not really the case.

But I am jumping the gun. In 1931, Scoil Bhríde moved from Pembroke Road to 19, Earlsfort Terrace. The Department of Education bought the house, and UCD, for some reason, donated the furniture. It was a large Georgian house, with spacious rooms which could accommodate the large classes (two classes to each teacher, when I was a pupil in the 1960s). It also had a big mews at the back gate on Hatch Lane, which was known as Tír na nÓg, where the '*báibíní*', as we called them, were taught—far away, as it seemed to them, from the big school.

The house in Earlsfort Terrace apparently seemed like a suitable premises in 1931. By the end of the 1950s, it was anything but. The huge, high-ceilinged rooms were heated by inadequate open fires. The walls had not been painted in decades, and were covered with (interesting) damp patches. The floors were bare, rather like fashionable floors these days, but they looked dismal then. We were constantly ill with colds and sore throats and a myriad of ailments, and no doubt this was partly due to the poor conditions. It was an uncomfortable place for a child and it must have been very depressing to be a teacher in that place.

Poor conditions were commonplace in schools in the early 1960s. However, it was clear to me even as a child, visiting the other big national school in the area, St Louis', in Rathmines, that ours were particularly bad. The romance of the old house was lost on me, as I shivered in the dark classrooms, or ate lunch in the gloomy basement, where we were served with hot water for our Oxo cubes or cocoa by Ellen, a very old lady who did all the cleaning and catering, and whom we liked although we were overawed by her age. Old people looked so ancient then—women had very straggly white hair, and wrinkled faces, which of course they never have nowadays. I am guessing that Ellen was not all that much older than I am now. The toilets—outdoor, of course—were a nightmare.

This is what Dublin Corporation inspectors thought too, when they visited in 1960. The house was judged to be dangerous, and in December 1960 the school was ordered to close down by March 1961. The main difficulty was that there was no fire escape, but it was not the only problem.

Donn Piatt, in his excellent article on the history of the school, 'Gearrchúntas ar Stair Scoil Bhríde', describes succinctly and objectively what happened at that juncture. But no amount of objectivity can eliminate the drama from the account. The manager of the school was the UCD chaplain. He was abroad at the time of the crisis and it fell to the parents' committee, Cáirde Scoil Bhríde, to handle it. They had three months in which to find a new premises. The Department of Education refused to give them a penny to renovate 19, Earlsfort Terrace. Why? It was 1961, the time of the demolition of Georgian Dublin. Knocking down old houses seemed to be a national priority. Perhaps in this instance the Department was right: the house was not and never could be appropriate as a school. But it should not have been demolished.

The Department agreed to pay for a site but it was up to the Committee to find one—a most bizarre situation, but, as we know, such situations still occur today. Once again, a friend in a high place, in this instance the Minister for Finance, James Ryan, suggested that the school try to acquire Cullenswood House. I have read two versions of how this acquisition was accomplished. According to the first, Senator Margaret Pearse donated Cullenswood House and its grounds to the nation, on condition that it be used to promote Irish culture. Donn Piatt's version is less romantic and probably more accurate. He writes that the Department of Education bought the house and grounds from Senator Pearse.

Whatever happened, Scoil Bhríde got its site, the Office of Public Works built the new school, designed by Louis Brennan, and in 1965 we all moved from the Terrace to Oakley Road. The official opening took place in 1966. President de Valera and Bean de Valera cut the ribbon at the gate and the pupils lined the drive in a guard of honour, as the presidential couple and Louise Gavan Duffy made their way slowly up to the schoolhouse, a little vignette in the chain of Irish history. I don't know why it took so long to build and fit out—or how we managed to stay in a condemned building without a fire escape for five years. Perhaps they built a temporary fire escape. I cannot recall.

Most of my schooldays were spent in 19, Earslfort Terrace. The teachers then were Bean Mhic a tSaoir, Iníon Uí Dhonnchadha, Bean Uí Shé, Bean Uí Mhurchú, Iníon Uí Ghacháin, Bean Mhic Ghiolla Rí and towards the very end, Bean Uí Chléirigh. In addition there were the aforementioned H. Dip. students, Miss Medlar, an elegant lady always wearing stiletto heels and a fur coat who taught us Irish dancing and a little gentle gym, and her long-suffering assistant Doreen Barnes, herself a past pupil of the school.

Doreen was always rather sardonic, in the nicest possible way, as she shouted out '*a haon dó trí ceathar cúig sé seacht, a haon dó trí, agus a haon dó trí*' (the fundamental rhythms of Irish dancing) for the millionth time. She startled us all when we went to a Christmas show at Miss Medlar's Dancing School and saw her transformed to a glorious ballerina, in black tulle tutu and pink pumps. How extraordinary that a teacher, even a dancing teacher, could look beautiful!

Scoil Bhríde pupils started school in the mews at the back of Earlsfort Terrace, on the lane where Mrs McCabe had her sweetshop to which we thronged on the way home, for pennyworths of pineapple chunks or sweet potatoes, scooped into paper cones. Bean Mhic a tSaoir, from Kerry, who had been teaching in the school since its foundation in 1918, presided over this end of the school, at one time called Tír na nÓg. She had a grandmotherly appearance when I started in 1959, and, like a grandmother, she was soft and kind. Her task was to teach us to speak Irish, and she did, more or less. Like many of the pupils, I did not really know Irish when I started school, although my father was a native speaker from Donegal. My mother did not speak Irish, though, so I just had a smattering.

My father's dialect was very different from any I encountered in Scoil Bhríde, where the teachers came from Kerry, Galway and Mayo. Never anyone from Donegal (or not in my day: one of the original teachers in 1918 was a certain Éilís Ní Dhuibhne, who must have come from Donegal, like almost everyone called Ó Duibhne). But I became fluent, like almost all the pupils, quite quickly. We really did speak Irish all the time, without difficulty, and quite naturally. It was a great gift to receive so easily and one for which I am eternally grateful.

Bean Mhic a tSaoir also taught us to sing. Songs are a great way to learn any language, and its grammar: a handy reference work which you can store conveniently in your head. The first song was 'Fáinne Geal an Lae', a strange choice, maybe, for báibíní, but a song with an easy air, and lovely words.

> *Ar maidin moch*
> *do ghabhas amach ar bhruacha Locha Léinn*
> *An samhradh teacht sa chraoibhín tais*
> *Le lonradh te ón ngréin.*
> *Ag taisteal dom trí bhailte phort*
> *Is ar bánta míne réidh*
> *Cé gheobhainn lem ais*
> *ach an Cúlfhion deas*
> *Le fáinne geal an lae.*

Which translates like this:

> *Early one morning I wandered out*
> *On the banks of sweet Lough Laine*
> *The summer kissed the budding branches*
> *In the beaming sun's warm rays*
> *As I went my way through ports and towns*
> *On smooth and pleasant plains*
> *Who came to my side but the fair-haired maid*
> *At the dawning of the day?*

So we were introduced to the Irish poetic tradition of the aisling at the age of four. We also sang more childish songs, like 'Órá Órá Chailín', a lullaby for our dolls, and 'Tá dhá bhóín bhainne agam', a song about cows.

In High Babies we began to learn to read, only *as Gaeilge*, and to write. In 1960 we were still using the Gaelic alphabet, and I am glad to have caught that just before the change to the Roman alphabet. It is cheering, somehow, to remember that the first letters one ever wrote were in the Gaelic script, and which was soon to be abandoned, just like 19, Earlsfort Terrace itself.

The highlight of the school year was *Dráma na Nollag* which is still performed every second Christmas in the school. The dráma was always the same one, a nativity play by Dubhglas de hÍde, written by him for Scoil Bhríde, according to tradition. A day or two before we got out for the holidays this play was performed by the Sixth Class girls, and all the school would gather to watch it.

Good small children, who could be trusted to stay quiet for the half hour or so of the play's duration, were cast as angels, and sat in the crib in white smocks, with silver cake stands tied to the backs of their heads. I was a pathologically quiet child so I was an angel for two or three years in a row, until I grew too big. I was a giant when I was seven and angels around the crib had to be small. In Fifth Class you got to be another kind of angel, a larger, singing one, in the choir. Rigged out in nightgowns and silver haloes, Fifth Class sang 'Oíche Chiúin' and 'An Céad Noel', all the usual carols in Irish versions.

Sixth was the big year when you finally got to be in the play itself—if you were lucky. During a tortuous few days casting took place. There were not enough parts for everyone in the class and half would be in the choir—again. It was agony. I—still on the big side, but not outrageously so—got to be the First Shepherd. Not a dream role. The great roles in the play were not the Blessed Virgin, and obviously not St Joseph (just a step above the choir). They have hardly any lines. The play is dominated by two peasant women who gossip about what is going on, and everyone wanted to be one of them. But the First Shepherd at least was a speaking part, with a reasonable amount of lines. I took it very seriously, dressed in blue slacks (my first slacks— trousers for girls had just come in), an Aran sweater, and a pillow case tied with string around my head for that authentic biblical look.

By then we were in the *scoil nua* on Oakley Road, and performing on a proper stage, and were heavily made up by Bean Uí Chléirigh, who was very artistic, and very optimistic. 'Why did you look like a clown?' the little boy who lived next door asked, to my disgruntlement. It was true that my face had red and yellow and blue stripes on it but the idea was that these would transform me to a weather-beaten shepherd, under the stage lights. Instead I looked like a war-painted Red Indian who had turned up in Bethlehem, pretending to be a shepherd. However, somebody's mother said I was born for the stage, which made me very happy indeed. I took that to be the objective review and ignored the little boy's comment.

My school days in Earlsfort Terrace were far from unhappy and in many ways inspiring, although I have some dark memories of the dim damp rooms, and a few teachers who slapped us with rulers far too often, for minor misdemeanors. That is how it was and it is hard to forgive retrospectively. Indeed I did not accept it at the time and found it humiliating and unjust. And terrifying. How could they? Some teachers were more violent than others, and some pupils were more beaten than others. I am certain there are people who have bad memories of the school. I was one of the lucky ones, protected somehow, as many were—by their parents, by their personalities, by their strategies for staying out of trouble. But no child should have to contend with institutionalised daily violence. And, no matter how romantic a picture one wants to paint of Scoil Bhríde, the truth is that it, like many schools into the 1960s, was a place where children were mistreated as a matter of routine. That was Ireland, in those days.

The move to Oakley Road changed everything. We left behind the gloom of Earlsfort Terrace, and came to the brand new, purpose-built building in Ranelagh. There were trees in the garden. There was grass. There were many airy warm classrooms, furnished with lovely desks and chairs, wood with coloured trims, blue, and yellow, green and red. Big wide blackboards on the walls. There was a kitchen, where Bean Uí Chléirigh taught the big girls to make strawberry buns and potato soup. There was the magnificent *halla*, with its real stage and magical velvet curtains, dark blue—what joy to be up on that, doing *Dráma na Nollag*, and later my own ghastly play, 'Baldy's Surprise' co-written by me and my friend Clíona Ní Fharrachtáin and performed for the school, under the direction of one of the amazing nuns from the H.Dip. course in UCD (who had expected, I know, better, but had commissioned us to write and had to grin and direct what she got).

That year, the year of the move, everything happened. In September 1965 the new school opened. At Easter 1966 we commemorated 'Éirí Amach na Cásca', (the 50th anniversary of the Easter Rising) like everyone else in Ireland. For the first time we in Scoil Bhríde learnt songs in English, so we could sing along with all the other Dublin children—'All Around my Hat I Wear a Tri Coloured Ribbon Oh', and 'The Bold Fenian Men', all of those. At Easter we marched with the primary schools to Croke Park, singing our heads off, and then sat through the seasonal pageant, the *Glóir Réim*. Indeed it was probably triumphalist and simplistically nationalistic, as its critics have said. But for us 12–year-olds, it was above all an inspiring and fantastic drama. I did not rush into the IRA after it, but I did want to rush into the theatre and see more plays and pageants.

That was my last year in Scoil Bhríde. We did the scholarship exam at Easter, and many of us got it, and we went off to our secondary schools. We had moved, in my childhood, from an old, tired system, impoverished and drab, into a brave new world, where there were velvet curtains on the stage, bright furniture in the classrooms, and strawberry buns in our bags as we went home.

Many of the girls went on to Scoil Chaitríona, Eccles Street, although many went to other schools too. The connections continued. Some of those girls went on to teach in gaelscoileanna, to start the new gaelscoileanna. Others, of course, went into all the walks of life which were going to open up for girls just as we emerged from secondary school five or six years later. We had been born at a lucky time in Ireland, especially if you happened to be a girl.

Scoil Bhríde in those days inculcated '*tír ghrá*'. There is no doubt about that. Its foundation stone was not political but cultural and linguistic patriotism. '*Ní tír gan teanga*' ('No country without a language') was the daily mantra. That speaking Irish was more virtuous than speaking English was certainly drummed into us. It is what many people firmly believed, in the 1960s, when Irish speakers had good reason to be defensive, since they were coming under serious attack from the Language Freedom Movement.

I do not think that we, the children of Ranelagh, Rialto and Rathmines, had any difficulty in accepting that English was the language of the city and Irish the language of the school. I do not think we seriously swallowed everything we were told. We knew it was perfectly possible to be bi-lingual, and probably realised that the official aspiration of the school, that Irish would become once more the language of Ireland, was nonsense, like so much else that we heard from our elders and betters. On the other hand, we knew that Irish was not sinister or evil, as some people in Dublin seemed to think. Scoil Bhríde taught us to be comfortable in two languages, and to aspire to know more. This alone was a great gift for any school to bestow on its pupils.

That we were fully conscious of being an important detail in the chain of Irish history was an additional bonus. Scoil Bhríde—which was far from perfect—opened doors to language and history. To the receptive student, this was a rich offering. The school—handicapped as it was by lack of facilities, poverty, and stultifying teaching practices—transcended its limitations. It fed and freed the imagination.

Scoil Bhríde continues to thrive. Under its principal, Iseult Ní Chléirigh, daughter of the wonderful Bean Uí Chléirigh, it is now one of the most popular gaelscoileanna in Dublin. It has 300 pupils, boys and girls, and every year receives applications from many more children than it could possibly accommodate.

For their generous and ready assistance with this article, I would like to express my gratitude to the principal of Scoil Bhríde, Iseult Ní Chléirigh and to the scholar, Elaine Sisson.

How Cullenswood House was saved

Ruairí Quinn

The first time that I became aware of Cullenswood House and its perilous condition was in 1984. The Ranelagh Branch of the Labour Party published a regular newsletter. Their March edition had a front page banner headline HISTORIC HOUSE UNDER THREAT.

Like many people, I was aware of the existence of Scoil Bhríde on Oakley Road and its connection with Scoil Éanna, the pioneering school which had been founded by Pádraig Pearse. My family lived in 70 Moyne Road, Ranelagh when I was born. Malachi Quinn, my father, had moved to Dublin in 1939 from Newry where he had grown up. John Quinn, my nationalist grandfather, had sent his third son, my father, to Scoil Éanna for a year. However, the connection between Cullenswood House, Scoil Éanna and my early childhood on Moyne Road only came together when the danger to this historic building was publicised.

The successful campaign to highlight the plight of Cullenswood House and ensure its survival and renaissance is a good example of local community activism and national political co-operation.

By 1987 Cullenswood House was empty, deemed unfit for human habitation and surplus to the requirements of its owners—the Office of Public Works. The new minority Fianna Fáil government had embarked upon an austerity programme to confront the difficult economic circumstances which faced the country and its economy. A number of corrective measures were announced by Finance Minister Ray McSharry including the sale of certain assets and properties. The semi-derelict Cullenswood House was among them.

The Belgrave Residents' Association had become aware of the threat to the historic house and launched a local and national campaign to save the house from being sold by the State. The prospect of its sale and demolition galvanised a dedicated group of local residents who were determined to alter the path of history. They were an alliance of Irish language enthusiasts, heritage defenders, conservationists and community activists who shared a common goal despite, or indeed perhaps because of, their different political allegiances.

The campaign was set up by the late Herbert Egan of Annesley Park, who died in 1991. Other members were Mícheál B. Ó Cléirigh (Rathgar Road) who succeeded Herbert Egan as Chairman, Mícheál Mac Gréil (Sandford Road), Pádraigín Uí Ghuidhir and Séamus Mac Ghuidhir (Merton Drive), John Baker (Oakley Road), Mairéad Uí Fharachtáin and Uinsionn Ó Farachtáin (Merton Drive), Monica Clune (Marlborough Road) Áine Ní Dhubhghaill (Oakley Road), Lillie Bennett (Annesley Park), Máire Davitt (Albany Road), Jim Connolly Heron (Oxford Road), Liam Ó hOisín (Glasnevin), Una Hayes and Bridie O'Donoghue (Killeen Road). Support for the campaign was sought and found from local political parties. The first task was to stop the sale of the building. I was asked to help.

Just why was Cullenswood House so important?

The first records date back to 1759 when Bartholomew Mosse, the founder of the Rotunda Hospital, is said by some to have died there, though this is disputed by Deirdre Kelly. The house stood in its own grounds and was unrelated to Oakley Road, in that it originally faced away from the road. It represents a house of an earlier time before the suburban streets were developed and when Dublin city was surrounded by country villas.

It is probably the oldest surviving building in Ranelagh. It is certainly Ranelagh's most historic building for two separate reasons. Cullenswood House was owned by the grandfather of William Lecky, the famous Victorian historian, whose statue stands in Trinity College. A liberal Unionist, he felt strongly about the distortions and slurs cast by English historians upon Ireland and devoted much of his energy to refuting them. The Lecky Library in Trinity College is a testament to his scholarship and commitment to Ireland. Perhaps it is that legacy which connects him to the next famous owner of Cullenswood House.

Pádraig Pearse acquired the property in 1908. He wanted to establish a new progressive boys' secondary school devoted to developing a love and knowledge of the Irish language and its culture. Teaching would be bilingual and the lay management of the school would be modern and liberal by the standards of the day. Pearse was excited by the potential of the building and wrote:

> Cullenswood House is situated in the healthiest part of the southern suburbs of Dublin, in a neighbourhood which combines rural amenities with the advantages of close proximity to the city. The Clonskea, Palmerstown Park, Dartry Road and the Lansdowne Road to Kenilworth Road tram lines all pass within three minutes walk of the gate. The Rathmines and Ranelagh Station of Dublin and South Eastern line are within one minute's walk. The grounds, which command a delightful prospect of the Dublin Mountains, include a lawn, a flower garden with vinery and conservatories, a vegetable garden, an orchard, a playing field, a handball court with an open air gymnasium.

Two years later, Pearse moved Scoil Éanna from Cullenswood House to Rathfarnham because of the success of his school project and the rapid increase in numbers. Four teachers from Scoil Éanna fought in Easter Week 1916: Con Colbert, Tomás MacDonagh, Willie Pearse and, of course, Pádraig Pearse. I do not think that any other school could claim such a distinction. In 1910 Cullenswood House became a school similar to Scoil Éanna, but for girls. Scoil Íde was established. Louise Gavan Duffy, one of its teachers, went on to establish Scoil Bhríde in St Stephen's Green, Ireland's first girls' gaelscoil.

In 1960 Senator Margaret Pearse, Pádraig's sister, bequeathed Cullenswood House and its grounds to the state. A modern school to accommodate Scoil Bhríde was built in the gardens of Cullenswood House in 1965. The new school building had a central role in the Irish language movement and its educational offshoot, the gaelscoileanna. In 1987, it was proposed to sell off Cullenswood House which was a derelict building, in order to raise finance for the Fianna Fáil government.

On 12 May 1987, at the request of the Restoration Committee, I raised the issue in the Dáil by way of a parliamentary question. This is how the record reads:

> Mr Quinn asked the Minister for Finance if he will lease Cullenswood House, Oakley Road, Dublin 6 at a nominal rent to a local conservation group, on condition that they restore the building, be responsible for its maintenance and upkeep, and make it available for community and cultural purposes including a permanent museum devoted towards the commemoration of the Irish Language Movement and its history; and if he will make a statement on the matter.

Minister for Finance (Mr MacSharry): The future use of this property is currently under review and I expect to arrive at a decision shortly.

On 4 June 1987 I again raised the matter in the Dáil with Noel Treacy TD, the Minister of State with responsibility for the Board of Works. Below is an extract from that debate:

Ruairi Quinn, TD: The State has effectively two options. The first is the option which the State proposes to exercise and that is to sell it and dispose of it. I would put it to the State and the representatives of the State, the Minister of State for the OPW, Deputy Treacy, that there is another and better option. The purpose of sale is to derive some asset value from this building. It is probably worth no more in the open market than approximately £50,000 [€63,500] and that is before the real hidden charges that Dublin Corporation now propose for connections to water and sewerage services.

. . . I would like to put to the Minister of State formally the following alternative proposal: that the OPW on behalf of the nation, exercising their functions within the jurisdiction of this State would make this building available at a nominal rent on a long lease to a community-based group whose intention would be to establish a museum devoted to the history of the Irish language movement and its cultural revival; that that building would be opened to the public and as part of the cultural infrastructure of this city would enhance the tourist attractions that Dublin needs in the advent of its millennium and coming in to the last 13 years of this century; that in addition it would become an important educational tool for many children of this generation who fail to see with the same degree of clarity of former generations the relevance of learning and speaking their own national language.

I went on to cite examples of work done with the help of AnCO (now FÁS) in refurbishing old buildings of cultural merit with the Community Youth Training Programme:

. . . there would be a museum devoted to the history of those people who had struggled to rescue from what seemed to be oblivion a language now vibrant and alive. We are aware of the politics of that struggle, perhaps in a partisan way. We are not aware, certainly our children are not aware, of the extraordinary steps and strides taken at different times over the long 100 years that elapsed since that movement got off the ground. There is nowhere on this island one can take a visitor and say: within the four walls of this building you will see encapsulated the history of that struggle and the fruits of that success.

Minister Noel Treacy was gracious in his response and outlined his own position:

I am pleased that Deputy Quinn has afforded me an opportunity to refer

Cullenswood House viewed from Oakley Road in the 1980s.

briefly to the situation pertaining to Cullenswood House in Ranelagh. Approximately two weeks after my appointment in the Office of Public Works the file on this matter was referred to me. I studied it, feeling that this historic property should be scrutinised by me, an inspection and report having been furnished already by the expert staff in the Office of Public Works. Cullenswood House is situated in Oakley Road, Ranelagh, and is at least 150 years old. It was acquired by Pádraig Pearse in 1908 and housed the first Scoil Éanna, Pearse's bilingual school for boys, from its inauguration in 1908 until its transfer to Rathfarnham in 1910. In that year, Pearse founded Scoil Íde, a bilingual school for girls in Cullenswood House . . . he also rented property across the road from Cullenswood House, popularly known as Sunnyside. Cullenswood House, as a bilingual school for girls, closed down in 1912. We are fortunate in the Office of Public Works to still have the lease Pearse signed in 1908, surely a very important artefact and museum piece.

Noel Treacy maintained his close interest in this project and finally persuaded his senior colleague, Minister Ray McSharry, to hand over the building to the Cullenswood House Restoration Committee on terms and conditions very similar to what had originally been proposed. While there was much political support for the project, Noel Treacy deserves pride of place for making the critical decision to save the building.

A lot of time elapsed between the decision in principle by Noel Treacy and the actual handover. The Cullenswood House Restoration

Committee was grateful for the help of officials in the Office of Public Works who ensured that the Department of Finance did not have second thoughts.

At last, in 1989, a 21-year lease with a nominal rent was agreed. The Restoration Committee got effective control of Cullenswood House. However, they had custody of a building that was in a serious state of disrepair. Some essential works needed to be done immediately. Money was now a priority. A Restoration Fund Appeal was launched in the Oak Room of the Mansion House in April 1991 by the Lord Mayor, Councillor Michael Donnelly. A target of £350,000 (€444,000) was set and the launch attracted a lot of publicity. Councillor Michael Donnelly had been Fianna Fáil's local representative for many years, representing the area with energy and enthusiasm.

Photographed at the launch with the Lord Mayor was Freda Egan, widow of the Cullenswood House Association's first Chairman, Herbert Egan, Fr Mícheál Mac Gréil, Treasurer of the Association and Mícheál B. Ó Cléirigh who succeeded Herbert as Chairman.

In 1991 the Restoration Committee obtained a government grant of £120,000 (€152,000). By 1996 they had raised £35,000 (€44,500). This enabled them to complete phase one of the development plan which included a new roof, structural repairs, the eradication of damp and the provision of new floors and ceiling structures. A Committee Room was completed to a high standard, together with a caretaker's apartment which was needed for security purposes.

Phase two of the development plan involved raising further funds as the proposed grant from Minister Michael D. Higgins, TD in the Department of Arts, Culture and the Gaeltacht required at least £30,000 (€38,000) in matching funds. The priority of the Restoration Committee continued to be to provide community access on an ongoing basis at the earliest possible opportunity for lectures, seminars of local cultural and historical interest, meetings for residents' associations, literary readings and workshops.

Around this time the Restoration Committee was approached by a group of parents who had applied to the Department of Education to establish a new gaelscoil called Lios na nÓg. This was because there was a shortage of places in the existing Scoil Bhríde and a growing demand for gaelscoil places in the community. Lios na nÓg proposed

The Cullenswood House Restoration Committee: (back, left to right) John Baker, Séamus Maguire, Liam Ó hOisín, Uinsionn Ó Farachtáin, An tAthair Mícheál MacGréil, James Connolly Heron (front, left to right) Máire Davitt, Áine Ní Dhubhghaill, Padraigín Uí Guidhir, Breandán Ó Cléirigh, Lillie Bennett, Máiréad Uí Fharachtáin.

to rent a number of rooms in Cullenswood House on a temporary three-year basis. In the meantime, they would be looking for permanent accommodation in their own right. The Restoration Committee was conscious that the rent that Lios na nÓg would pay for the classrooms would help towards financing the second phase of the development plan.

However, things did not work out as originally intended. Funds were difficult to raise. Lios na nÓg was growing rapidly. More rooms were rented to the school. The Restoration Committee had a debt of over £108,000 (€137,000) in the local AIB bank with little prospect of clearing it. They were half way through their 21-year lease and were fearful for the completion of the original project.

The building unit of the Department of Education and the Board of Lios na nÓg opened discussions with the Restoration Committee. The proposal was to turn Cullenswood House into a permanent home for Lios na nÓg. The option was to surrender the balance of the lease to the Department of Education with the agreement of the Office of

Public Works in return for clearing all the debts of the Restoration Committee. This was reluctantly agreed. The handover to Lios na nÓg and the Department was completed in January 2001. In April 2001 the Restoration Committee dissolved the Cullenswood House Association.

The original objective of saving Cullenswood House was achieved. The building has been modernised and enlarged to provide a permanent home for Lios na nÓg. It is, perhaps, fitting that just 100 years after Pádraig Pearse purchased Cullenswood House it will now contain Scoil Bhríde in the gardens and Lios na nÓg in the old, now refurbished, building of Cullenswood House.

The wider objective of a community resource for lectures and seminars of cultural interest as well as workshops and literary readings could not be realised. The continued demand for such activities does require all of us to look at how we make the best use of our communal facilities such as schools, halls, churches and libraries. The completion of the new permanent building will enable Lios na nÓg to consolidate and develop its own cultural and community activities. I am aware that the Cultural Committee of Lios na nÓg has run cultural events including two historic lectures on Scoil Éanna and held a public debate on what constitutes a Republic. No doubt the management of Lios na nÓg will use Cullenswood House to build upon these activities. The community contribution of Ranelagh's Multi-Denominational School, which this year celebrates its 21st anniversary, is an example which could be developed.

Some members of the original Restoration Committee have passed away, others resigned prior to its dissolution, unhappy with the direction of the project. But all can take considerable pride in achieving what they set out to do in 1987.

Cullenswood House has been saved. A modern gaelscoil will take up residence within its walls and the sounds of children playing, laughing and learning will continue to be heard around Oakley Road. The alternative prospect, nearly realised in 1987, was another apartment block—the last thing that Ranelagh needed or wanted.

I hope that somewhere in the refurbished building space will be found to tell its history and to remember the members of the Restoration Committee whose dedication ensured its survival.

The plaque commemorating the re-opening of the house by Minister Éamon Ó Cuív in 1997.

Site visits: A conservationist's notes on the challenge of Cullenswood

Peter Pearson

I first visited Cullenswood House in 1986, when I was very active in the Dublin city branch of An Taisce, and there was talk of demolishing the buildings there. Demolition of historic buildings and houses was a major problem in the 1980s, and few people concerned themselves. State agencies and public bodies were no better than the developers.

However, all that changed during the 1990s and Cullenswood House, Rathfarnam Castle, Dublin Castle and Lucan Garda Station became some of the first examples of the State's new interest (albeit under pressure) in architectural conservation.

Cullenswood could have easily been swept away. Not that it was of outstanding architectural interest, but it had considerable character and perhaps more importantly, was part of the higgledy-piggledy Georgian charm of Oakley Road—a winding street of interesting and attractive detached and terraced houses. Indeed, several important Georgian houses nearby were demolished at this time.

Cullenswood House, a late Georgian house built originally on Cullenswood Avenue, was the largest detached house in the immediate area. The street name was changed to Oakley Road in the mid-19th century, following the gradual development or 'infill' of the houses on the rest of the road. Certainly some of the houses on Oakley Road date from the latter half of the 18th century, including an attractive Georgian terrace of houses which were knocked down in the mid-1980s.

In 1833 a Charles Joly sold Cullenswood House to John Lecky, a barrister, from Portarlington, Co. Laois. The Dublin street directory shows that in 1839 he was resident in Cullenswood House. This was the grandfather of the famous historian and politician, William Hartpole Lecky. Though William Lecky was a Unionist, Patrick Pearse was later impressed by the association when he founded Scoil Éanna in the house in 1908. He wrote in his school journal of 1909, 'So our school-house has already a very worthy tradition of scholarship and devotion to Ireland, not indeed founded on so secure and right a basis as ours, but unwavering, life-long.'

Pearse asserted that William Lecky was born in the house, but he was actually born in his parents' home, Maesgwylldd House in Blackrock, Co. Dublin. His father sold Cullenswood ten years after the historian was born, in 1848, so it is possible that he visited it as a child.

A Mrs (Colonel) Vincent is listed, during the same years—perhaps the house was divided or sub-let.

By 1850 the house is listed as 'vacant' in Thom's *Dublin Directory*, and was again vacant in 1876. In the last two decades of the 19th century (1884 and 1894 *Directories*) the house is occupied by William Jeffares, a tea, coffee and spice merchant, with a business address at 76 Thomas Street, sharing premises with Baker Wardell, who were also noted general merchants.

George James Patterson sold the house to Patrick Pearse on 7 August 1908 for £370. The sale included 'woodlands'. By 1917, and again in 1921, we find Mrs Pearse in Cullenswood House.

In 1960 the State took ownership of the house from the Pearse family. It was allowed to fall into gross disrepair.

In 1986, it was hard to see its potential, as the ground floor windows had been sealed up with concrete blocks and the whole place was neglected. In 1990 I visited the house again with my friend Monica Clune, who was a member of my committee at Drimnagh Castle Restoration Project, and Micheál Mac Gréil and prepared the following short report.

Observations

1. Cullenswood House is at present a poor advertisement for itself: its windows are blocked up, the rooms inside are therefore dark and cannot be fully appreciated. There is rubbish strewn about, the grounds are messy.

Cullenswood House in the 1980s—note the wooden props on the west wall.

2.Having said this, the charm of the house is still apparent, and when returned to its former glory it will be a graceful and elegant 18th-century house, evocative of its historic and dignified past.

3. Nearly all old buildings present problems and Cullenswood has its share of them. However, it is basically a structurally sound house which has in general been well maintained. The roof is in reasonable condition.

4. Architecturally, the house does not pretend to be in the same league as Rathfarnam Castle or the Casino. But it is a typical example of the type of house which is becoming more and more uncommon. It has several fine features: the bow with its original curved windows, an attractive hall, good plasterwork of the 1880 period, all of which is intact. The house contains all of its original windows and panelled shutters; and the staircase is intact. In short, the house merits careful restoration even if it were not for its important historic associations.

5. Like most 18th-century houses, Cullenswood has been added to at least twice. Some of the additions might be expendable, others might

prove invaluable as a caretaker's house or later as offices, kitchen etc.

6. One of these extensions is the source of a structural problem at the south-west end of the main house. At some time an additional 6 to 8 feet were added (at three levels) to the end of the original house. Poor foundations or settlement has caused this section to subside and pull away.

7. Another addition includes a central landing and hall, to the south-west and rear of the main house. Water penetration through this top hall has caused a limited amount of rot and collapse of plaster and floor here. The tarred roof of this section is in poor shape.

8. The last addition is the 19th-century section at the rear. This section is in good condition and the roof appears to be sound.

Recommendations

1. A philosophy of restoration should be adopted. The European approach is to do the minimum that is necessary to bring the building back into use and back to its former glory, at the same time not losing its feeling of age and elegance. This means retaining old plaster finishes (not just decorative details), all old floorboards, all original joinery, shutters, doors, windows and staircase. Apart from respecting the character of the house, this also means saving money. Too often an architect or engineer will specify the removal of all these features, or they may be lost through careless site supervision. (A new pair of Georgian sliding sash windows and frame will cost between £300 and £400 each). A programme of work could be established which would involve protecting these features from the outset.

2. I believe security is very important and that the Victorian addition mentioned above in (8) should be converted as a caretaker's flat immediately, before any work commences on the main house.

3. Depending on financial resources and on the envisaged end use I would suggest that the addition mentioned in (6) could be removed altogether. The original windows and roof would have to be re-instated but a large problem area would be removed.

4. Similarly, the extension including the hall to the rear mentioned in

(7) could also be removed. This would involve careful planning and some rebuilding around the staircase but it would also eliminate a number of problems. However, as this hall might later prove useful it is a decision which would merit careful thought.

5. Main house: the main roof could be strengthened and repaired rather than being replaced at great cost. Even the attic room has distinct character which evokes the mood of the writer's study. This would be destroyed if the roof were rebuilt. All of the house has great atmosphere and potential, and a sensitive restrained hand is needed if this is not to be replaced by a sterile replica. Unfortunately, some of the best panelled doors and all of the mantelpieces were removed when the house was vacant. However, it is still possible to find identical examples or even have them made up. The house may be of fine brick construction underneath the cement render.

6. The scale of the restoration of Cullenswood House is not daunting. It is manageable. But as a voluntary undertaking it does require the assistance of Government agencies and Dublin Corporation.

The rescue of Cullenswood is a challenging project which will add just one more dimension to the cultural richness of Dublin.

Observations on my return, 2009

Cullenswood House is a late-Georgian structure (c.1800) with substantial Victorian additions to the rear. The main house, with its distinctive bow end, facing Oakley Road, stands two storeys over basement. A granite string course separates the basement and ground floor. The arched opening of the main entrance is approached by a flight of granite steps. There may once have been a decorative fanlight over the hall door but it is now plain. The original multi-panelled hall door has survived, along with part of the wrought iron handrail on the steps.

Inside, the hall is ornamented with a decorative plaster ceiling divided into three compartments by a band composed of interconnecting roundels, and a small wreathed centrepiece.

To the right is an attractive room, now an office. The office, with

The new north entrance, part of the extension between the old house and Dr Boylan's house.

its bowed shape, is probably part of an early extension, but it contains all its original architraves, shutters, and Georgian chair-rail and dado. A reeded cornice is typical of the Regency style of c.1800.

Across the hall is a large drawing room, possibly extended or created by joining two smaller rooms together.

Cullenswood House has been very carefully restored, with original features preserved or replicated where necessary. The Georgian sash windows have been reconditioned and, combined with the new exterior lime render, has restored the original elegance of the house and brought it new life. It also demonstrates that a school can operate in an historic building which combines the best of old and new.

Surrendering history

Alan Gilsenan

Every house has its ghosts, every home its history. The silent echoes of lost lives. Their sorrows and their sunlight.

Outside this particular house, the sun falls fleetingly upon a goldfish pond. It is carved, perhaps, of silken granite, sculpted by some long-forgotten stonemason. Down amongst the murky water and the pondweed, small slivers of gold glisten and shimmy in the light. It is now the late 1950s and a small boy looks down upon this early morning scene from a window high in the house. He is filled with a strange sense of awe and wonder. The boy will remember this image of the goldfish pond, down there, in the Coolings' garden, for the rest of his livelong days. It may call to him, even, in his final hour.

He is walking now, that boy, up the stairs of the old house. Each

The last residential years—Scoil Bhríde (opened in 1966) is just visible to the left, as are the decorous lace curtains on every window.

step seems to fall away from him, seemingly giving way inward and downward towards the dark stairwell, towards the bannister rail upon which he must have once slid down with shiny-pants swiftness. He is a man now, the boy, nearly fifty years on, and his footfall heavier now than of old. He walks up through a kind of dusty twilight, although it is still bright outside. Past peeling paper and tattered curtain. For the boy is coming home, at last.

For a moment now, perhaps, he imagines that he hears a distant rumble on the Harcourt line. His ghost mother calling up as she bustles down past them upon the stairs, struggling with the baby brother's pram. *Come on, Ciarán, or we'll miss the Bray train.* Possibly he remembers the excitement of that journey to the sea, the end-of-the-line station, the Majestic Hotel tucked into the shadow of Bray Head at the end of the promenade. He recalls also playing with his brother on the deserted bandstand, aloft on its vast horizon. Senses once again the longing gaze of the old gentlemen squinting out from behind the curtain netting of the boarding houses that line the promenade, their sea-scoured walls of flaking pastel paint bestowing upon them a kind of Continental elegance. These memories too, glimpsed amidst the sparkle of boyhood, harked back to the grandeur of a more glorious time. Even then, it seems, the hand of the past glories lay heavy upon them.

He pulls himself back from this eerie reverie, and continues upstairs. With him on the stairs are his father Noel and his younger brother Paddy. (They have come at the invitation of Gaelscoil Lios na nÓg to excavate their past under the prying eyes of some new-fangled, and unsettlingly small, video camera.) Here they are then, returning to the small flat that was home to them, the Scarletts, all those years ago. They pause for a moment on the upstairs landing, their eyes adjusting to the gloaming. Around them now, they can see the forgotten debris of classrooms. The toppled child-sized chairs, discarded copy-books, the crayon drawings in all their primitive wonder. Beautiful bright young faces shine out of the photographs stuck to a cardboard Celtic cross still Blu-tacked to the wall. A wash of colour and hope scattered there amongst the early evening gloom. But there is a sense, too, in all these abandoned relics of abrupt departure, of a sudden absence, of children gathered up into the arms of strong, capable women and ushered swiftly to safety.

But this is not what the Scarletts have come to find. They have come in search of their own remembrances, to try and reclaim the ghost of themselves. Before it is too late, before the great gods of refurbishment descend upon the house bringing gifts of re-wiring and re-plumbing, of green energy and tasteful design. For soon, light will come flooding fast into this gloomy sepulchre and these shadows will be banished forever.

They push on down the corridor, past the spot where once stood the trellis gate that marked the entrance to their part of the house. It is gone now, of course, but the old skylight remains above and casts a shadowy light upon the peeling wallpaper. It has a distinct and somewhat regal Celtic design, quite unlike the bedsit patterns that fall and flap off other walls. Ah, that'll be one of the originals, Noel comments with a quiet reverence, I remember that alright.

He is there now. Beside them. The Mister Pearse. The workman pauses to take a deep satisfying pull on a Sweet Afton and surveys his new handiwork. 'Looks well, Mr Pearse.' 'Indeed and it does, Tommy. Indeed and it does,' replies Mr Pearse and hurries off downstairs to the kitchen where Margaret has some fresh tea brewing. MacDonagh was due shortly too, bless him. What would we do without him? For the year is 1908 and all the plans for the new school are falling nicely into place.

And it was this Margaret— 'the Miss Pearse'—who let Cullenswood out in flats half a century later before it all fell into rack and ruin. Senator Margaret Pearse (as she would be by then) was Noel Scarlett's godmother so she made sure that Noel and his young family got a decent sized flat: a small kitchen-cum-parlour, two bedrooms and that part of the landing, of course, that lay beyond the trellis. There were others too about the house: the Donnellys ('Charlie had three daughters'), the Misses O'Connor, the Holloweds, the Joyces ('Helen Joyce would later marry Terry Wogan, from the television, you know'), and the Nugents, of course. Fifteen of them alone on the Scarletts' floor and only one toilet between the lot of them.

And, of course, the old sisters Cadiz with their cats down beyond in the basement. A whole host of them. The Burmese and the Siamese and the odd Persian, the moggies and tabbies. And a damnable nuisance they were too.

The boys remembered the cats alright. Fluffy balls of them. And other things too. Other fragments. All the jaded beauty. The broken fanlight above the door. The sash windows and the half-shutters. The boarded-up fireplace. Wet days stuck indoors. The blue and white gas cooker. Those gas taps. The endless warnings from their mother about those taps. *Never, ever, turn on those taps, never. Ciarán, do you hear what I'm after saying?* The smell of gas about the flat. The whiff of sulphur. The struck match and ring taking hold. The kettle boiled. The tea made.

And walks out to Palmerston Park and down by the Dodder, watching out for mallards and herons and the odd clutch of white swans. Following it all the way down to Ballsbridge. And, above all, the great copper green dome of the Church of Mary Immaculate glimpsed through ragged autumn trees and from the topmost windows. Rathmines Church, the Refuge of Sinners. *May perpetual light shine upon them.*

There was talk also. Idle banter. Hushed mentions of Mr Pearse. The family connections, the blood line. (The Scarletts were descended from the progeny of Mr Pearse senior's first marriage to Emily, who passed away at a young age leaving behind Patrick's half-siblings little Mary Emily and James.) People said that Patrick Pearse had a squinty eye, a glass eye even, that Pádraig Mac Piarais who died for Ireland. Dying for Ireland, well, wasn't that something grand? Something to be proud of? The blood of the martyrs and the adoration of the Cross. These were things to venerate, heads bowed in the dark in humble supplication. *To thee do we cry, to thee do we send up our sighs, mourning and weeping in this valley of tears.* The boys remembered his steely profile hanging in their classroom alongside the Pope in Rome and President Kennedy in America. But, later, talk of their famous ancestor started to recede. The boys sensed a kind of embarrassment take hold of their story. A sort of deep unease. What with the North and everything. *Everything.*

There were stories too. The old stories, the intoxicating ether of the nation. Tales from the Eamhain Macha. Of Fionn MacCumhaill and the fiercesome Fianna. The legends of the Tuatha De Danaan. Distant dreams of Cúchulainn dying for Ireland. The Hound of Ulster. That twisted naked torso and the amputated stump of a pillar. A raven perched upon his shoulder. The motherless child. *The gift of sorrow.* And Christ too died on the Cross for our sins. To save mankind. *Who fears to speak of Easter Week? That week of famed renown.*

These were grand stories to be told and re-told. To be remembered. And Mr Pearse built a theatre for the boys out there in the garden. With good solid walls and a corrugated iron roof that beat like a tomahawk on a Red Indian's drum when it rained. But there were fine red velvet curtains inside and coloured lights above the stage, and Mícheál Mac Ruaidhrí, the gardener, had put up a trellis of sweet peas on the outside which certainly took the bare look off the place. And so here, in the grounds of Cullenswood House, great dreams were dreamed and the young and the beautiful kept faith with those dreams.

Later, some people would laugh at these dreams. Pour scorn upon them. But what did those people know? With their small minds and petty imaginings? They knew nothing. Nothing of glory and longing, nothing of the great potency that these dreams held hidden deep within their imaginary fire.

Back in the 1940s, Noel Scarlett too had dreamed of glory of a kind and had joined the FCA, the Pearse Battalion, of course, although today it is known as 'D' Company. *'Beart do réir armbriathar.'* That came back to him perhaps as he wandered through the old house. *'Beart do réir armbriathar.'* There was a real sense of doing something for your country then as well. Marching up and down, up and down, each and every Sunday morning up at the Portobello Barracks, dressed in all your finery. Every Easter Sunday, they would gather together and march in double quick time down the Grand Canal to Pearse Street (could you believe it?) and over to Parnell Square and the Garden of Remembrance. How proud Noel Scarlett must have felt marching past the GPO, knowing that a little precious Pearse blood was coursing through his veins.

It irked Noel a bit when the Irish government suspended the Easter Sunday commemorations in the early 1970s. Some of his old friends from the FCA felt the same way. 'What did any of them know? They were surrendering history, they were,' he commented as they stood again on the darkened landing, at home now and at ease with the place once more. Here, in the dim light, Noel felt comfortable now here in the old place. Had reclaimed it somehow for himself. He could hear, once again, its faint and lonely music and the old tune seemed to come alive inside him once more.

That music drew them towards one last unopened door on the landing. More of a cupboard really than a door, it seemed. A secret entrance. A long-forgotten stairway perhaps. So up they went, Noel and the boys. *You'd want to mind your step here, especially in the dark.* The attic was low and smelt of damp. In the murky light, they could hear a faint scratching. A rat perhaps? Or a trapped bird? Who really knew the truth about a house's inhabitants? Those who dwelt in the unknown and dark contours of its geography.

'This is where we kept the turf and briquettes,' Noel remembered. The boys remembered too and opened a small window-like door out on to the roof. They crawled out and stood beneath the moonlight looking out towards the city. In the distance, they could see the silhouette of Rathmines Church and, beyond that, perhaps even the red warning light atop the Millennium Spire. It was quiet now, high up there above Oakley Road, up with the gods that watched over the comings and the goings below. The three men stood in silence and let the night settle about them.

'Vampire jets,' said Ciarán suddenly. 'Vampire jets. I remember the roar of them.' During the 1950s, the boys would have stood up here each Easter Sunday morning as their father marched proudly down O'Connell Street. They would stand here on the roof and listen for the distant noise of the crowd. Then, to crown it all, they would eventually hear what they were waiting for—the roar of Vampire jets as they swooped in and low over Dublin's city centre and on down, down the length of the parade below. And then, just as suddenly, they would be gone, an eerie trail of smoke evaporating over Dublin Bay. *Did you see the Vampire jets, Mammy?* Ciarán would ask.

Far below them now, on the threshold of the hall door, stood Mr Pearse, stiff-backed in his black teacher's gown. The night was calm. The sky was clear. He had perhaps heard the distant roar of the Vampire jets beyond and now he stood looking quizzically up at the stars. *What mysteries did those heavens hold? What promise lay beyond those stars?*

Behind him, lining the dark emerald-green walls of the elegant hallway, hung class photographs of the boys of St Enda's. Brave sons of Erin. Fine Gaelic teams and the drill units. There were photographs and posters taken from the plays and the pageants of the recent terms. *Íosagán. The Lost Saint. The Coming of Fionn.* These heroic children of

Lir, these child warriors, his beautiful wingéd boys ascending into the burning light of the heavens.

It had been a good year or two, he thought, all in all. He had forged a fine school right here in this fine house. His lads were now far beyond the dead hand of the Murder Machine. (He regretted that phrase now, it seemed a bit melodramatic, perhaps? How much he had learned about this politics game, although he knew well that the hard men of the organisation still thought him naïve.) Nonetheless, the promise of a noble future lay ahead for each and every child who had passed through this house. But perhaps we have outgrown Cullenswood? Something bigger possibly would suit our purpose better, out in the countryside beyond the city? *Whist awhile, Paddy, why do you always crave something more? Are you not content here? Now?* Yes, he thought, I am content here. Now. Happy even, perish the thought. *Happy*, how strange it sounds, that word. *Happy*.

One of the cats brushed against his trouser leg and made its unhurried way out into the night. Down in the basement, he could hear his sister Margaret bustling about making the last pot of tea of the day. This day, the ninth day of April, 1909.

Patrick Pearse lifted his face towards the sky. He felt the soft spring breeze gentle upon his cheek. He closed his eyes and smelled the air, fragrant and full now with the scent of freshly-mown grass. The first cut of the season, Mícheál had reminded him. He opened his eyes. The night was beautiful. Clear. The stars seemed almost within his grasp. They seemed to be calling out to him. Calling him home.

'A mháthair,' arsa Eoghainín, 'tá siad ag glaoch orm. "Teara uait go dtí an tír a mbíonn an ghrian ag soilsú i gcónaí ann—teara uait, a Eoghainín, thar na farraigí fraochda go dtí tír an tsolais—teara uait a Eoghainín na nÉan!"'

A voice called to him from deep within the house. The boy paused for a moment and then turned and stepped back into Cullenswood House, its stately hall door closing silently behind him and upon all those that dwell within.

Aisling gheal: The founding of Gaelscoil Lios na nÓg

Róisín de Buitléar

The letters fell onto the doormats in January 1996. All around Ranelagh parents were informed that their four year olds had not been accepted for the local all-Irish school that coming September.

Scoil Bhríde had been long established as the gaelscoil in the area. The letter offered a list of other gaelscoileanna in the locality which included Scoil Mológa in Crumlin, Scoil Naithí in Nutgrove, and Scoil Lorcán in Stillorgan. I rang them all. They were all a car journey away, they were full, and they all had waiting lists. At the same time as I had received my letter, a number of parents of pupils of the pre-school class attending Scoil Bhríde heard that they were not to have a place there either. Being denied the chance to have an education through Irish both angered and frustrated parents but it was to be the spark which ignited the project to set up a school of our own.

The catalyst was Gréagóir Ó Dúill, a poet, aided by his wife Cáit, a teacher, Ranelagh residents who are part of the Irish-speaking community here. They are the grandparents of a child who had been hoping to attend Scoil Bhríde that September. Cáit had been entrusted by her daughter to handle all the arrangements for little Sorcha who would be returning home from a number of years in Russia just in time to grab her school bag and pencil before the first day of school. Cáit had even got as far as discussing the type of shoes required with the school as everything had to be arranged long-distance. They were assured they had a place and the news to the contrary came as a complete shock to them.

While Gréagóir was wandering around Ranelagh fuming, he happened upon his neighbour Ailbhe Ní Chaiside, Professor of

The house as it looked when Lios na nÓg moved in.

Phonetics at Trinity. Ailbhe shared his indignation, having suffered the same fate for her daughter and enthusiastically responded to Gréagóir's suggestion of getting involved in setting up a school of their own. Ailbhe became the first chairperson of the Lios na nÓg board and a continual inspiration. Her unfaltering 'we will make it happen' attitude carried us all through many hurdles on our journey.

Gaelscoileanna is an organisation which provides advice and practical support to communities which choose to establish an Irish-medium school. They were the essential link between all of us who were floundering with how to solve our children's schooling dilemma. Initially they put us in contact with each other and later provided the knowledge we needed on how to approach the project and what steps we were to follow and in which order. Twenty was the magic number. We required 20 four-year-olds who had not previously been registered for school in Ireland, whose parents wanted them to be educated in the Ranelagh area, through Irish. We also needed a location for the school, a teacher and a three-year waiting list of similar aged children with like-minded parents to have any chance of getting recognition for our school as a State-paid national school.

We were living in one of the most expensive areas for real estate in Dublin, house prices were on the increase, school sized land was scarce, prices were exorbitant.

Our first task was to fill the classroom with potential pupils. Convincing first-time parents to sign up for a school with no history, no premises, no facilities, no teacher, with education through Irish at its core, narrowed the field somewhat. First-time parents were an important part of the picture as generally children have secured a place in a school if the older sibling is already attending. With eight primary schools in the immediate area this fact swallowed a lot of potential candidates. We needed courageous parents who dared to be different.

Film-producer Nuala O'Connor and musician/broadcaster/film-maker Philip King had a bigger problem than we had at that time. They had three girls, triplets who had no school places. Eveleen Coyle and Fergus Mulligan were in a similar boat with school-less twins. That made five for the list already. Gaelscoileanna put enquiring parents in touch with Gréagóir and Ailbhe, and Nuala and Eveleen got to work mustering support, and finding children.

They started with the Scoil Bhríde pre-school class. Slowly the list grew. It was decided to hold a meeting to inform the public, publicise the idea and extend our list of school-goers. About 60 people turned up, the atmosphere was charged. We collected more names for that coming September and a sizeable list of possible school entrants for the forthcoming years. A solid body of committed parents emerged, amongst them Celine Darcy, a district nurse who joined the set-up committee.

Amongst the parent body of the original class was an inspiring group of parents for whom Irish was significant in their lives. Many of them were native speakers, many had a deep interest in Irish culture, language, music, and literature and wanted to nurture and explore this with their children. Some parents had no Irish, one was Swedish, one was English. Some wanted their child to love Irish and not to experience the difficulties and loathing they had experienced while learning it themselves. There was a belief in the success of a total immersion system, a school that was really committed to teaching through Irish and making Irish the working/playing language used every day. There was a great energy amongst this group, where everyone had something they could offer. Everyone was welcomed and valued for what they

School's over! And Louis Ó Laighin, Martina Ní Raghallaigh and Aoife Meates are off for home.

could bring to the project. There was a great sense of community and a real feeling of people doing something to help themselves. 'Local', 'community' and 'family' were key words that describe this time. There was so much to be done.

Formidable women in the group tackled the politicians in the area and the campaign to get a possible location and temporary recognition status for the school began. Frances Fitzgerald (Fine Gael), Ruairí

Quinn (Labour) and Eoin Ryan (Fianna Fáil) came to our meetings; they really listened and lobbied on our behalf. Meetings were held in the kitchens and sitting rooms of our homes. People were dispatched to hunt out any possible sites—disused buildings or land lying idle. Every old church or empty building became a potential venue which had to be investigated. We had insider knowledge within the parent base and used every lead we had. It was exhausting.

Through political connections we secured the old nurses' home at the Royal Hospital, Donnybrook on a year's lease. It was a stand-alone building surrounded by tall trees, grassy lawns and a car park. It was idyllic from the outside, bright and airy inside, with room to expand. It had been unused for many years. It was filthy and needed painting. We didn't care. We pulled the parents together and organised a swat team of cleaners and painters. I learned things about cleaning standards that evening that I had never known before. Nurses and air hostesses in rubber gloves have a superior standard of cleaning and a hunter's instinct for seeking out dust behind cast iron radiators. This was the first time many of us had met as parents and we all still laugh and remember that evening as one of great hilarity and of realisation of what we had all taken on.

Deciding on a name for the school was another defining moment. The word '*lios*' means an enclave or protected place. It is pronounced 'liss' as in 'kiss'. It came from discussions on raths and local place names. '*Na nÓg*' means belonging to young people. There are thousands of lioses dotted around the country which are mounds of earth often surrounded by trees which are associated with folklore, fairy people, magic and music. Folklore warns against their removal or destruction.

We felt we were on the brink of something new, a school with fresh ideas, creativity and challenges that would reach new communities and look forward, something to nurture, a safe place for our children to learn. Seán Ó Casaide, Ailbhe's father, a retired school teacher and inspector from Gaoth Dobhair, came up with the final version. It is fitting that a man who nurtured so much within the Irish-speaking community in Ranelagh can be credited with that. Lios na nÓg became the name and later the inspiration for the logo of the school. The logo, designed by my husband, Terry Greene, draws on the lios

Áine Nic an tSíthigh, Principal of Lios na nÓg since 1996.

form and sun motif. We wanted a bright happy image which set us apart from the conventional idea of a school identity. It conveyed the idea that what was happening inside the school would radiate to the community outside.

The logo was applied to the school jumper that first year and only became compulsory when the parents opted for a school uniform in the third year. The T-shirts were introduced in the summer term and the multi-coloured T-shirts, now so much part of the school, came about because the supplier in Spiddal couldn't get the original colour and offered a series of colour choices. Instead of choosing one the principal opted for the lot.

We planned to start the school with one class, junior infants. We needed to find a teacher for this class but also knew that whoever this teacher would be would also become the principal and shape our school in the future. Employing Áine Nic an tSíthigh was the most important action we took in the journey of this school. She is quietly spoken, from Fionntrá in the Kerry Gaeltacht with a wry smile and that Kerry knowingness about her that can be formidable. She was very experienced and was looking for a fresh challenge. She had a vision for the kind of school of which she wanted to be principal: a country school in the city in which Irish was central, one which involved parents or grandparents in the classroom, one which really respected tradition and nurtured culture, one in which teachers were as important as the pupils, one in which music, drama, art, dance, sport, language and culture formed part of everyday activities.

It was a vision of a school that could be shaped and formed by the team and the parents, which allowed learning to happen at a pace that was right for the situation and included everyone, regardless of their standard of living or education. She wanted a school that respected nature and the environment and above all one that had a happy, open atmosphere. It sounds idyllic but it was also our vision. We needed a visionary leader: when we engaged her we had no money to pay her. She has delivered on all this and more.

With the appointment of the principal, a school board was formed. Ailbhe Ní Chasaide was chairperson, and the other members were Gearóid Mac Unfraidh, Nuala O'Connor, Eveleen Coyle, Gréagóir Ó Dúill, Róisín Ní Ghuidhir, Áine Nic an tSíthigh and myself, Róisín de Buitléar. The school opened in the Royal Hospital nurses' building in September 1996.

We had 20 students, although one was under age. On that first register were: Naoise Nic Eochaidh, Chloe Nic Uiseannáin, Niamh Nic Unfraidh, Clár Ní Mhaolagáin, Sorcha Ní Dhubhghaill, Síofra Ní Luain, Caoileann Ní Dhúda, Siobhán Nic Colla, Molly Nic Giolla Bhríde, Ellen Nic an Rí, Juno Nic an Rí, Molly Nic an Rí, Caitlín Ní Chaisaide, Conchúr Ó Maolagáin, Pádraig Mc Carthaigh, Cúan Ó hÚaine, Aaran Craobhach, Aindrias Ó Caoimh, Samuel Maolalaidh Ó Connachtaigh, Ben Ó Lennáin and Marcas Ó Dorchaigh.

By that time we had achieved a status of temporary recognition for the school. This meant we could pay the principal, and order school supplies, but we didn't have any school furniture in that first week or month. Everyone brought their own little chair from home and we cobbled together tables and desks. We started the class library by everyone bringing a story book from home on that first day to put on the shelf, a practice we kept up for a few years. Again, the parents stepped in to act as classroom assistants each day as we had no budget for that. Within the first week the kids were coming home with songs and chants in Irish, and were killing themselves laughing that the donkey in their reader was also called Áine! In Lios na nÓg the teachers are known by their first names. Noirín Ni Chatháin joined us in the second year. She was very young, bubbly, energetic, easy going, and fresh to teaching. She is from the Aran Island of Inis Oirr. Muinteoir Noirín brought her own charm to the school, much of it centred around humour and the rich cultural heritage she wears like a layer of her skin. She became the vice-principal, Áine's co-driver and constant team mate.

In that second year we also established Naíonra Lios na nÓg, the pre-school led by Cherrie Uí Bhroin. This was and continues to be the first step in the Lios na nÓg experience. The much-adored 'Cherrie's' is a haven for preschool children. Her endless patience, gentle ways and introduction to learning Irish through creative exploration sets the tone for how the child learns in the big school.

Within the second year of the school we were in real trouble as to where we were going to find the money or the land on which to build the school. The Royal Hospital was looking to recover the building we were in, for its own purpose. We now had two classes and a pre-school with another class coming on stream in September. We had to find suitable premises quickly! Róisín Ní Ghuidhir, who was active with Lios na nÓg from the beginning, knew of the Cullenswood restoration project being undertaken by local residents. Her mother Pádraigín was a key motivator in this project. Pádraigín knew that their ability to raise funds and to restore the building as a cultural centre was losing momentum. Lios na nÓg approached the Cullenswood House Committee to see if we could rent the building as a location for the school. Our proposal was that with this state-guaranteed rental income the committee could take out a loan to continue the restoration project and realise their dream of seeing the house reinstated as an important historical building. Eventually, the plan was accepted and work started in the house to bring it to a standard safe to house children for the forthcoming year. It was, in truth, a very risky move.

The roof had been restored and one room in the front of the building was suitable as a classroom. The rest was in disrepair and the second floor was very unsafe. The yard was small, but the atmosphere was just what we wanted, a great big welcoming hall door, a big house for our small school that everyone could reach on foot. The historical significance speaks for itself. We called on more parents to plant the garden with plants from home. The yard was made safe. The upstairs was sealed off. In 1999 we moved in with three classes and the Naíonra. History was making a full circle. Negotiations started with the House Committee about the possibility of the school taking on the responsibility of the future of the house full term.

From the start, the school body has involved the wider community in its activities. The wider school community sees itself as central to cultural issues and events in the area. Over the years, concerts, workshops and evening classes have been held in the school, not only for the children and parents but for the public too. It makes no sense to Lios na nÓg that a school building should be closed for many months of the holidays or the weekends when it could be used for other events during these periods. The door is always open to the public to events held within the school year. With this idea in mind, the proposal was made to approach the committee with a view to transferring ownership of the house from the Office of Public Works to the Department of Education to house the school permanently at Cullenswood House. This would mean we would have a permanent location and the House Committee would have a guarantee that the school would keep alive its vision as a cultural centre in Ranelagh. It also meant that the Department of Education would get a fine, very expensive piece of land and building for a school they were now compelled to house, for free. Pearse must have been rooting for us because the committee finally agreed to hand the building over. Today, 12 years on, as I wait for my daughter to emerge from the warren of prefabs that temporarily house our school while the renovation of Cullenswood is taking place, I see hundreds of children scattering towards their parent or grandparent or minder. I never fail to be amazed at what a group of parents continues to achieve by working together.

Lios na nÓg would never be the school it is now without the extraordinary dedicated teaching staff and the team that Áine Nic an tSíthigh steers daily, which includes the staff, parents and children. The past pupils I asked are fiercely proud of their school which they remember not as an institution but as a big family gathering in which you just happened to learn. Every parent who ever signed a child up for this school and committed him- or herself to strengthening this project can take heart that their action has created layers in a community which will continue to enrich and enliven Ireland's culture and language for the future.

Aisling Gheal: Bunú
Ghaelscoil Lios na nÓg

Róisín de Buitléar

Bhí na litreacha á seachadadh i mí Eanáir 1996. Bhí scéala faighte ag tuismitheoirí éagsúla nach raibh áit dá bpáistí a bhí ceithre bliana d'aois, sa ghaelscoil áitiúil i mí Mheán Fómhair dar gcionn.

Bhí Scoil Bhríde ina gaelscoil sa cheantar le fada an lá. Moladh do na tuismitheoirí áiteanna a lorg i nGaelscoil Mológa i gCros an Araild, i Scoil Naithí i mBaile an tSaoir, agus i Scoil Lorcáin sa Charraig Dhubh, sna litreacha seo. Chuir mé glaonna orthu ar fad agus bhí siad

Na naíonáin sínsireacha ag súgradh, 2007—tá an logo ar an mball.

Bunaíodh an naíonra sa dara blian.

píosa maith ó bhaile agus iad lán agus iad ag tógáil ainmneacha do liostaí feithimh.

Thart ar an am seo, fuair roinnt de thuismitheoirí naíonra Scoil Bhríde scéala nach raibh áit acusan ach oiread i rang na naíonáin bheaga. Chuir an easpa deise seo oideachas a fháil trí Ghaeilge fearg agus frustrachas ar thuismitheoirí ach ba é a chuir an lasóg sa bharróg, le gaelscoil nua a bhunú.

Ba é Gréagóir Ó Dúill, file, agus a bhean chéile Cáit, múinteoir, an nasc a bhí leis an tionscnamh—beirt a bhí ina gcónaí i Raghnallach agus a bhí mar dhlúthpháirt de phobal labhartha na Gaeilge anseo. Bhí garpháiste acu féin a bhí ag súil le tosú mar dhalta i Scoil Bhríde an Meán Fómhair úd. Ba é an dualgas a chuir a hiníon ar Cháit nó na socraithe cuí a dhéanamh dá garpháiste a bhí le filleadh ón Rúis le tosú láithreach bonn ar a céad lá ar scoil. Bhí Cáit ag fiosrú faoin gcineál bróga a bheadh ag teastáil don scoil ó tharla go raibh a hiníon i bhfad ó bhaile agus bhí dearbhú tugtha dóibh cheana féin go mbeadh áit ann don pháiste. Bhí ionadh an domhain orthu nuair a dúradh leo ansin nach mbeadh áit dí i Scoil Bhríde.

Nuair a bhí Gréagóir ag spaisteoireacht thart ar Raghnallach lá agus é breá tógtha faoin scéal, tharla gur casadh a chomharsa Ailbhe Ní Chasaide, Ollamh le Teangeolaíocht i gColáiste na Tríonóide air. B'amhlaidh cás a bhí ag Ailbhe nach raibh áit dá hiníon Caitlín i Scoil Bhríde ach an oiread. Eatarthu beirt shocraigh siad gaelscoil úr a bhunú agus ba í Ailbhe céad chathaoirleach Lios na nÓg. Thug sí spreagadh leanúnach don ghrúpa bunaithe agus bhíodh sí i gcónaí dóchasach go n-éireodh linn an beart a dhéanamh cé go raibh mórán constaicí inár mbealach.

Tugann an eagraíocht Gaelscoileanna comhairle agus tacaíocht phraiticiúil do phobail gur mian leo bunscoileanna trí mheán na Gaeilge a bhunú. Ba iad an nasc a bhí riachtanach le muid uilig a aontú leis an fhadhb scolaíochta dár bpáistí a réiteach. Ba iad a chuir na tuismitheoirí éagsúla i dteagmháil lena chéile i dtosach báire, agus ba iad a chuir comhairle orainn faoi cén bealach tabhairt faoin tionscnamh agus faoi na céimeanna a bheadh riachtanach a ghlacadh

Ag súgradh.

agus leag siad ord na gcéimeanna sin amach dúinn.

Ba é fiche an uimhir dhraíochta. Bhí orainn liosta d'fhiche páiste ceithre bliana d'aois a chur le chéile, páistí nach raibh cláraithe do bhunscolaíocht riamh cheana in Éirinn agus gurbh é mian a dtuismitheoirí go bhfaighidís oideachas trí mheán na Gaeilge i gceartlár Raghnallach.

Bhí suíomh de dhíth don scoil, múinteoir lena dteagasc agus liosta feithimh de pháistí den aois chéanna a bheadh ag teacht ar ball agus tuismitheoirí a mbeadh suim acu sna haidhmeanna céanna linn le go mbainfimis aitheantas dár ngaelscoil mar Scoil Náisiúnta a bheadh íoctha ag an stáit. Bhíomar inár gcónaí i gceann de na ceantair ba dhaora tithíochta agus talún i mBaile Átha Cliath. Bhí luachanna na dtithe ag méadú, bhí suímh do scoileanna gann agus bhí na luachanna thar fóir.

An chéad chuspóir a bhí againn ná an seomra ranga a líonadh le daltaí. Bhí sé ródheacair tuismitheoirí a earcú do scoil a bhí gan stair, gan fhoirgneamh, gan áiseanna, gan mhúinteoir agus bhí an cineál oideachais a bhí beartaithe sainiúil—oideachas trí Ghaeilge, rud a bhí cúng go leor. Ba iad na tuismitheoirí a raibh a gcéad pháiste ag tosú ar bhunscoil a ba mhó a raibh muid dírithe orthu toisc áiteanna a bheith faighte ag paistí ní ba óige i mbunscoileanna dá mba rud é go raibh deartháir nó deirfiúr ag freastal orthu cheana féin. Bhí cuid mhaith de na páistí tógtha cheana féin toisc go bhfuil ocht mbunscoil sa cheantar. Bhí muid ar thóir tuismitheoirí cróga a bhí sásta a bheith difriúil.

Bhí fadhb mhór ag an léiritheoir scannán Nuala O'Connor agus ag a fear céile Philip King. Bhí trírín cailíní acu agus gan aon scoil acu dóibh. Bhí cúpla ag Eveleen Coyle agus Fergus Mulligan agus ba amhlaidh an cás dóibhsean. Bhí cúigear páistí ar an liosta faoin tráth seo. Chuir Gaelscoileanna tuismitheoirí a bhí ag tosú i dteagmháil le Gréagóir agus le hAilbhe agus thosaigh Nuala agus Eveleen ar thacaíocht a lorg agus ainmneacha páistí a bhailiú.

Thosaigh siad le páistí ó naíonra Scoil Bhríde agus níorbh fhada gur mhéadaigh an liosta. Socraíodh ar chruinniú poiblí a scairteadh leis an bpobal a chur ar an eolas agus poiblíocht a thabhairt don smaoineamh agus cur le liosta na bpáistí. Tháinig thart ar seasca duine agus bhí daoine tógtha. Fuaireamar roinnt ainmneacha don Mheán Fómhair dar gcionn agus liosta sách mór do na blianta le teacht. Tháinig coiste chun cinn de thuismitheoirí dúthrachtacha agus bhí banaltra ina measc darbh ainm Celine Darcy.

Bhí baicle áirithe de thuismitheoirí spreagúla a raibh páisti acu sa rang bhunaithe gurbh í an Ghaeilge croílár a saoil. Ba í an Ghaeilge a dteanga dhúchais ina lán cásanna agus bhí suim mhór ag baicle eile sa chultúr Gaelach, sa Ghaeilge, sa cheol agus sa litríocht. Ba é a mian é seo uilig a chaomhnú agus a roinnt lena bpáistí. Bhí cuid de na tuismitheoirí gan aon Ghaeilge; Sualannach agus Sasanach ina measc. Bhí cuid acu gur mhaith leo go dtabharfadh a bpáistí grá don Ghaeilge gan na deacrachtaí agus an fuath a bheith acu a raibh taithí acu féin orthu don Ghaeilge agus iad ag foghlaim na Gaeilge ar scoil. Chreid siad go docht i gcóras an tumoideachais agus go n-éireodh leo scoil a bhunú a mbeadh an teagasc go hiomlán trí mheán na Gaeilge inti agus ina mbeadh an Ghaeilge ina teanga oibre agus shúgartha gach lá sa scoil.

Bhí a lán fuinnimh ag na tuismitheoirí seo agus bhí tallann éigin le tabhairt acu uilig don tionscnamh. Bhí meas ar gach tuismitheoir agus ar an tallann a bhí le roinnt acu. Cuireadh fáilte roimh gach duine agus bhí meas ar an méid a thiocfadh leo a thabhairt don tionscnamh. Bhí spiorad láidir pobail ann agus daoine ag cuidiú leo féin le rud faoi leith a dhéanamh. Ba iad na focail agus na coincheapanna ba thábhachtaí ag an am seo ná 'áitiúil', 'pobail' agus 'teaghlaigh'. Bhí obair mhór le déanamh.

Thosaigh mná láidre sa ghrúpa ag dul i bhfeidhm ar pholaiteoirí an cheantair agus an feachtas sa tsiúl le suíomh oiriúnach a aimsiú agus aitheantas sealadach a fháil don scoil. Fuaireamar éisteacht mhaith agus tacaíocht láidir ó Frances Fitzgerald (Fine Gael), Ruairí Quinn (Lucht Oibre) agus Eoin Ryan (Fianna Fáil) agus rinne siad freastal ar ár gcruinnithe. Reáchtáladh na cruinnithe céanna inár gcistiní agus inár seomraí suite féin. Cuireadh daoine amach ar thóir shuíomh i bhfoirgnimh fholmha agus ar thalamh a bhí díomhaoin. B'éigean gach sean-eaglais agus foirgneamh folamh a fhiosrú le fáil amach an mbeadh siad oiriúnach.

Bhí roinnt eolais ón taobh istigh againn i measc na dtuismitheoirí agus d'úsáid muid an t-eolas sin uilig. Bhíomar tuirseach traochta!

D'éirigh linn léas bliana a fháil trí cheangail pholaitiúla ar sheanáras na mBanaltraí san Ospidéal Ríoga i nDomhnach Broc. Ba foirgneamh

Carúil na Nollag, lá fuar gheimhridh.

leis féin a bhí ann le crainn arda agus plásóga glasa agus carrchlós thart air. Bhí sé go hálainn ón taobh amuigh agus é geal agus fairsing taobh istigh agus d'fhéadfaí cur leis. Bhí sé ina luí folamh le mórán blianta. Bhí sé an-salach agus é le péinteáil ach ba chuma linn. D'eagraíomar meitheal de thuismitheoirí agus buíonta tuismitheoirí le dianghlanadh agus péinteáil a dhéanamh.

D'fhoghlaim mé a lán rudaí faoi ghlantóireacht nach raibh ar eolas agam roimhe sin. Tá bealach faoi leith ag banaltraí agus aeróstaigh le lámhainní rubair de chaighdeán thar barr glantóireachta a dhéanamh agus deannach agus salachar a aimsiú ar chúl teasairí iarainn. Ba í seo an chéad uair dúinn casadh le chéile mar thuismitheoirí, agus is minic ó shin a rinneamar gáire agus muid ag smaoineamh siar ar an tionscnamh a ghlac muid orainn féin.

Ba rud faoi leith ainm na scoile a roghnú chomh maith. Tagann an focal 'lios' ó áit atá sábháilte nó áit atá dúnta isteach. Tháinig an focal chun cinn agus plé á dhéanamh ar ráthanna agus logainmneacha áitiúla. Ciallaíonn 'na nÓg' go mbaineann sé leis na daoine óga. Tá na mílte liosanna ar fud na tíre; ardáin thalaimh a mbíonn crainn thart orthu go minc agus a bhaineann le béaloideas, síóga, draíocht agus ceol. Coscann an béaloideas orainn dochar a dhéanamh dóibh nó iad a leagan.

Bhraitheamar go rabhamar ar tí rud nua, scoil le smaointe úra, samhlaíocht agus dúshláin a bhunú; scoil a thabharfadh tearmann do phobail úra, a bheadh nua-aimseartha agus a thabharfadh beathú agus áit shábháilte dár bpáistí le bheith ag foghlaim. Ba é Seán Ó Casaide, athair Ailbhe, iar-chigire scoile agus iar-mhúinteoir a chaith tréimhse fhada i nGaoth Dobhair a cheap an teideal deiridh. Ba thráthúil gurbh eisean a thug mórán spreagtha do chúrsaí Gaeilge i bpobal Raghnallach a fuair an t-aitheantas faoi cheapadh an teidil sin. Ba é 'Lios na nÓg' ainm na scoile agus ba é an t-ainm a thug an smaoineamh do lógó na scoile chomh maith.

Ba é Terry Greene, m'fhear céile, a chruthaigh an lógó atá bunaithe ar chruth leasa agus móitíf na gréine. Theastaigh íomhá, shona gheal uainn a dhéanfadh muid a idirdhealú ó na gnáthsmaointe a bhaineann le gnáthscoileannna. Ba é an smaoineamh ná go leathnódh obair na scoile amach i measc an phobail taobh amuigh. Cuireadh an lógó ar gheansaí na scoile an chéad bhliain agus ní dhearnadh éigeantach é go dtí níos moille, nuair a shocraigh na tuismitheoirí go mbeadh sé mar pháirt den ionar scoile. Cuireadh T-léinte leis an ionar do théarma an tsamhraidh agus tharla sé sin toisc nár éirigh le lucht déanta na ngeansaithe an dath céanna a fháil agus chuireadar réimse dathanna ar fáil. In ionad dath amháin a roghnú do na T-léinte roghnaigh an príomhoide an réimse iomlán dathanna.

Shocraíomar ar an scoil a thosú le rang amháin, na Naíonáin Shóisearacha. Bheadh múinteoir le roghnú agus thuigeamar gurbh é/í seo an té a bheadh ina phríomhoide/príomhoide amach anseo agus a bheadh i bhfeighil thodhchaí na scoile. Ba é ceapachán Áine Nic an tSíthigh an gníomh a ba thábhachtaí a rinneamar le linn an aistir seo. Ba as Baile an Fheirtéaraigh i nGaeltacht Chiarraí d'Áine agus cé go raibh sí séimh, ciúin, ina cuid cainte le meangadh beag ar a béal, bhí sí láidir ó thaobh pearsantachta mar is dual do na Ciarraígh. Bhí mórán taithí aici agus í ar thóir dúshlán úr. Bhí fís ag Áine den chineál scoile gur mhaith léi a bheith ina príomhoide uirthi; scoil thuaithe sa chathair ina mbeadh an Ghaeilge lárnach inti.

Bheadh áit do thuismitheoirí sa seomra ranga agus bheadh meas mór ar thraidisiúin agus dhéanfaí cothú ar an gcultúr. Bheadh an meas céanna ar na múinteoirí agus a bheadh ar na daltaí agus bheadh an ceol, an drámaíocht, an ealaín, an rince, an spórt, an teanga agus an cultúr mar pháirteanna de ghníomhaíochtaí laethúla na scoile.

Ba í an fhís go bhféadfaí an scoil a mhúnlú agus a chruthú tríd an fhoireann agus na múinteoirí le chéile agus go ligfí don fhoghlaim gluaiseacht ar an luas a d'oirfeadh do chách, ba chuma cén t-oideachas nó maoin shaolta a bheadh ag na páistí. Theastaigh scoil uaithi a mbeadh meas á thaispeáint ar an nádúr agus ar an timpeallacht ach a bheadh sona oscailte. Ba chosúil le Tír na nÓg í an áit seo ach ba í sin an fhís a bhí againn. Bhí ceannaire físe uainn agus nuair a d'fhostaíomar Áine ní raibh an t-airgead againn lena híoc. Ach tá sí tar éis an méid seo a chur i gcrích agus a lán eile lena chois.

Nuair a ceapadh an Príomhoide bunaíodh Bord Bainistíochta. Ba í Ailbhe Ní Chasaide a bhí ina cathaoirleach agus ba iad Nuala O'Connor, Eveleen Coyle, Gréagóir Ó Duill, Róisín Ní Ghuidhir, Áine Nic an tSíthigh, Gearóid Mac Unfraidh agus mé féin, Róisín de Buitléar, na baill eile a bhí ar an mbórd bainistíochta.

Osclaíodh an scoil den chéad uair i seanfhoirgneamh na mbanaltraí san Ospidéal Ríoga i Meán Fómhair 1996. Bhí fiche páiste againn cé go raibh páiste amháin ró-óg.

Ba iad na páistí a bhí cláraithe ar an gcéad ionrollacháin ná iad seo a leanas: Naoise Nic Eochaidh, Chloe Nic Uinseannáin, Niamh Nic Unfraidh, Clár Ní Mhaolagáin, Sorcha Ní Dhubhghaill, Síofra Ní Luain, Caoileann Ní Dhúda, Siobhán Nic Colla, Molly Nic Giolla Bhríde, Ellen Nic an Rí, Juno Nic an Rí, Molly Nic an Rí, Caitlín Ní Chasaide, Conchúr Ó Maolagáin, Pádraig Mac Cárthaigh, Cúán Ó hUaine, Aaran Craobhach, Aindrias Ó Caoimh, Samuel Maolalaidh Ó Connachtaigh, Ben Ó Leannáin agus Marcas Ó Dorchaigh.

Faoin tráth seo, bhí aitheantas sealadach faighte againn don scoil. Chiallaigh sé seo go raibh an Roinn Oideachais ag íoc as pá an phríomhoide agus as na soláithirtí scoile, ach ní raibh aon troscán againn sa chéad seachtain ná sa chéad mhí. Ba é an nós a bhíodh ag na páistí ná go dtugadh gach duine a chathaoir féin leo ón mbaile don scoil. Leanadh an nós céanna seo chun leabharlann na scoile a chnuasach. Thógadh na páistí leabhair isteach le cur ar sheilfeanna na leabharlainne, nós a leanamar sna chéad bhlianta. Ghlac na tuismitheoirí cúram maoirseoireachta sa seomra ranga orthu féin chomh maith, ceal airgid. Bhí na páistí ag teacht abhaile ag deireadh na chéad seachtaine le rannta agus amhráin as Gaeilge. Shíleadar go raibh sé an-ghreannmhar Áine a bheith mar ainm chomh maith ar an asal ina leabhar léitheoireachta!

Ba nós seanbhunaithe i Lios na nÓg na múinteoirí a ainmniú lena n-ainmneacha baiste. Tháinig an múinteoir óg fuinniúil, úr, réidh, Nóirín Ní Chatháin an dara bliain agus ba as Inis Oirr na Gaillimhe í. Thug Nóirín an dúchas agus an oidhreacht as ar múnlaíodh í léi go dtí an scoil agus bhí sé mar dhlúthpháirt di.

Ba ise an leas phríomhoide, leathbhádóir Áine agus ball foirne seasta dílis.

Bunaíodh Naíonra Lios na nÓg sa dara bliain chomh maith agus bhí sé faoi stiúir Cherrie Uí Bhroin.

Bunaíodh an Naíonra mar an gcéad chéim do pháistí roimh dhul go Lios na nÓg. Ba amhlaidh a bhí sna chéad bhlianta agus tá sé mar an gcéanna go fóill. Tá grá thar cuimse ag na páistí ar Cherrie agus is tearmann álainn é Naíonra Cherrie do na páistí réamhscoile. Tá foighne gan teora agus bealach séimh, bog ag Cherrie agus í ag plé foghlaim trí mheán na Gaeilge agus déanann sí fiosracht chruthaitheach na bpáistí a spreagadh agus a threorú mar thúschéim dá bhfoghlaim sa scoil mhór.

Tháinig fadhb mhór chun cinn sa dara bliain nuair a d'inis an tOspidéal Ríoga dúinn go raibh an foirgneamh de dhíth orthu féin agus go mbeadh orainn foirgneamh nó talamh a aimsiú go gasta. Faoin tráth seo, bhí dhá rang agus naíonra againn agus rang eile ag teacht i Meán Fómhair agus bhí orainn foirgneamh a aimsiú go pras!

Bhí Róisín Ní Ghuidhir gníomhach i Lios na nÓg ón tús agus bhí eolas ag Róisín ar an obair chaomhnaithe a bhí idir lámha ag pobal Thí Fhiodh Cuillinn i Raghnallach. Ba í máthair Róisín, Pádraigín, an ceann feadhna a bhí ag spreagadh agus ag stiúradh an choiste. Bhí a fhios ag Pádraigín nach raibh ag eirí leo an ciste airgid a bheadh riachtanach d'obair chaomhnaithe ar an teach mar Áras Chultúrtha a bhailiú. D'fhiafraigh Coiste Lios na nÓg den choiste sin an bhféadfadh Lios na nÓg an teach a fháil ar chíos don scoil. D'fhéadfadh an cíos seo ón stát cuidiú leis an gcoiste iasacht airgid a fháil chun an teach a chóiriú agus a chur ar ais mar fhoirgneamh tábhachtach stairiúil a bhíodh ann tráth.

Glacadh leis an phlean ar deireadh agus tosaíodh ar an teach a dhéanamh sábháilte go leor do phaistí óga scoile don bhliain scoile dar gcionn.

Cuireadh deis ar an díon agus d'fhág sin go raibh seomra ranga amháin ar thosach oiriúnach mar sheomra ranga. Bhí an chuid eile den teach i ndroch-chaoi agus bhí an dara hurlár an-dona agus dainséarach. Bhí an clós beag ach bhí an t-atmaisféar díreach mar a theastaigh uainn, teach mór dár scoil bheag. Bhí doras mór fáiltiúil ar thosach an tí, agus bhí sé cóngarach do dhaoine le siúl chuici. Ba léir an tábhacht stairiúil do chách.

Chuaigh tuismitheoirí linn le plandaí a chur as a ngairdín féin agus rinneadh an clós ní ba shábháilte do na páistí. Chuaigh Lios na nÓg isteach sa teach i 1997 le dhá rang agus an Naíonra. Bhí an stair beagnach curtha i gcrích go hiomlán. Thosaigh plé idir an dá dhream go bhfeicfí an dtiocfadh leis an scoil lán-fhreagracht a ghlacadh ar an teach sa todhchaí.

Bhí an scoil préamhaithe sa phobal máguaird ón tús maidir leis na gníomhaíochtaí a bhíodh ar siúl. Glacann an scoil lena ról lárnach i ngnóthaí cultúrtha agus imeachtaí sa cheantar. Cuireadh mórán ceolchoirmeacha, ceardlann agus ranganna oíche ar fáil ní hamháin do na páistí ach don phobal chomh maith. Is smaoineamh maith an scoil a bheith in úsáid le linn shaoire an tsamhraidh agus ag deirí seachtaine nuair is féidir imeachtaí breise a chur sa tsiúl inti. Bíonn fáilte roimh an bpobal ag na himeachtaí uilig i rith na scoile bhliana.

Socraíodh mar sin go ndéanfaí iarracht úinéireacht an tí a aistriú ó Oifig na n-Oibreacha Poiblí go dtí an Roinn Oideachais ionas go mbeadh ionad buan ag Lios na nÓg i dTeach Fhíodh Cuillinn, le dea-thoil choiste an tí. Chiallódh sé seo go mbeadh ionad buan againn agus go mbeadh barántas ag coiste an tí go mbeadh imeachtaí beo cultúrtha á reáchtáil i Raghnallach go rialta. Chiallódh sé go mbeadh píosa luachmhar talún agus foirgneamh ag an Roinn Oideachais saor in aisce chun scoil a reáchtáil ann. Caithfidh sé go raibh Pádraig Mac Piarais ag déanamh idirghuí ar ár son mar gur thoiligh an coiste an foirgneamh a thabhairt ar láimh dúinn ar deireadh.

Cuireann sé síor iontas orm an méid is féidir a chur i gcrích nuair a oibríonn tuismitheoirí as láimh a chéile. Bím ag machnamh air seo na laethanta seo agus mé ag fanacht le m'iníon dhá bhliain déag d'aois agus í ag teacht amach as cnuasach seomraí réamhdhéanta ina bhfuil Lios na nÓg lonnaithe go sealadach i láthair na huaire a fhad is atá cóiriú iomlán á dhéanamh ar Theach Fhíodh Cuillinn. Bím ag féachaint ar na tuismitheoirí, na seantuismitheoirí agus na feighlithe ag bailiú na gcéadta páiste a thagann as an scoil gach lá.

Ní bheadh an scoil mar atá sí inniu gan an obair chrua mhúinteoireachta a dhéanann an fhoireann agus na cúntóirí eile atá faoi stiúir laethúil Áine Nic an tSíthigh agus dar ndóigh na páistí féin. Tá ardmheas ag na hiardhaltaí ar Lios na nÓg agus ní chuimhníonn siad uirthi mar institiúid ach mar chlann mhór a tháinig le chéile chun deis foghlama a chur ar fáil dóibh agus gur fhoghlaim siad i ngan fhios dóibh féin.

Is féidir le gach tuismitheoir a chuir páistí chuig Lios na nÓg nó a thacaigh leis an tionscnamh seo a láidriú, a bheith bródúil agus sásta ina gcroíthe gur bhunaigh siad rud faoi leith sa phobal a leanfas ag spreagadh agus ag saibhriú agus ag caomhnú chultúr agus theanga na hÉireann sa todhchaí.

Gura fada buan í Lios na nÓg!

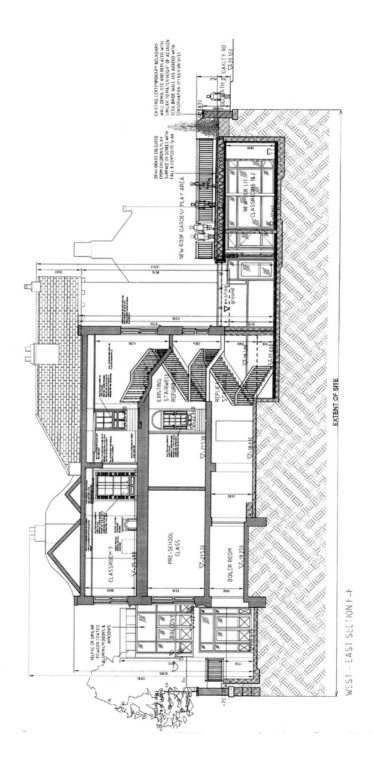

Architect's plan showing the new west–east section (from the front) with Oakley Road on the extreme right.

Restoring Cullenswood House:
An architect's progress report,
April 2009

Paddy Fletcher

Cullenswood House was semi-derelict in the mid 1990s and was saved by work carried out to the roof, some of the structure and on the lower ground floor. This work was organised by the Cullenswood House Restoration Committee. In 2000, A&D Wejchert & Partners were appointed by Gaelscoil Lios na nÓg to prepare a design for the refurbishment and extension of the house to accommodate the school. They needed eight classrooms and a number of ancillary rooms.

The appointment was made after a feasibility study was carried out, which established that it would be possible to accommodate the school at Cullenswood House and this was accepted by the Department of Education and Science.

The existing house is approximately 600 square metres in area. The standard Department of Education and Science brief for an eight-classroom primary school is 1372m^2. Due to the restricted site area around Cullenswood House and its urban character, it was not possible to accommodate all of that 1372m^2 area. A condition of the Department's acceptance was that Lios na nÓg would accept that not all the classrooms would be the normal 70m^2 each. The school was happy to accept this condition, bearing in mind the unique heritage of Cullenswood House. The school design was therefore prepared in which five classrooms and the ancillary accommodation will be located in the existing house and three classrooms and the school hall will be accommodated in extensions.

One extension is located to the north of the school in the space between it and No. 21 Oakley Road. This extension accommodates the

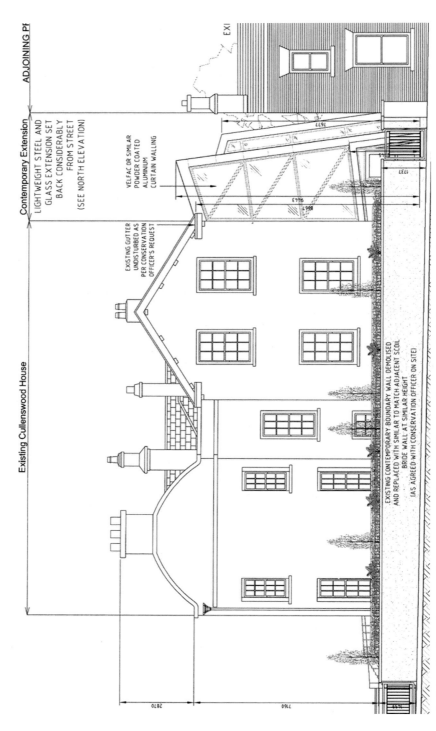

ADJOINING PI

EXI

Contemporary Extension

LIGHTWEIGHT STEEL AND
GLASS EXTENSION SET
BACK (CONSIDERABLY
FROM STREET
(SEE NORTH ELEVATION)

VELFAC OR SIMILAR
POWDER COATED
ALUMINIUM
CURTAIN WALLING

EXISTING GUTTER
UNDISTURBED AS
PER CONSERVATION
OFFICER'S REQUEST

Existing Cullenswood House

EXISTING CONTEMPORARY BOUNDARY WALL DEMOLISHED
AND REPLACED WITH SIMILAR TO MATCH ADJACENT SCOD
BRIDE WALL AT SIMILAR HEIGHT
(AS AGREED WITH CONSERVATION OFFICER ON SITE)

Architect's plan showing the new view from Oakley Road. Dr Boylan's house is on the right.

school hall at lower ground floor level, one classroom at upper ground floor level and also a new stairs and lift providing universal access to as many floor levels as possible, bearing in mind the level changes in the existing buildings. The roof of this area had to be tapered away from the boundary with No. 21 to ensure no greater overshadowing will occur to its rear garden than is already the case. Indeed it should be acknowledged that the development would have been very difficult to realise without the cooperation and patience of the owner of No. 21, Dr Peter Boylan. With his cooperation, it has been possible to demolish and re-build his front and rear garden walls, as well as install temporary diversion of his drainage during the works.

The second part of the new accommodation is to locate two classrooms between the house and Oakley Road. To be able to do this without screening the view of the house from the road, it was necessary to sink these classrooms into the ground and locate a small outdoor play area on the roof.

During the preparation of the tender documents, Lios na nÓg was in occupation of the ground floor and part of the lower ground floors of Cullenswood House. It was therefore not possible to open up large parts of the building to establish its condition at that stage. The rest of the building was semi-derelict with access to the second half of the lower ground floor almost impossible and no floorboards, ceilings or plaster at first floor level.

The design was developed through the various required Department of Education stages with cost checking being carried out and input from other consultants at each stage. Each stage had to be approved by the Department before the next could start. As the design developed and consultations took place with the Dublin City Council planner, conservation and fire officer, many issues arose which increased costs. Stage approvals were very difficult to obtain. The architects were assisted by White Young Green, Civil and Structural Engineers, Varming Consulting Services Engineers, Kerrigan Sheanon Newman, Quantity Surveyors and Jeremy Gardner Associates, Fire Consultants. Planning permission and the fire certificate were obtained with reasonable efficiency as a result of extensive pre-submission consultation.

Tender documentation was completed in late 2006 and tenders received in early 2007. Tenders were very competitive which reflected the market at the time. The contract was awarded to the lowest tenderer, Dunne Contracting Ltd. The competitiveness of the tender permitted the addition to the contract of the removal of the external sand/cement render off the building and its replacement with traditional lime render. This allows the building fabric to breathe. The contract started in April 2007.

Shortly after the contract was awarded, Dunne Contracting Ltd went into examinership. Whereas the examinership concluded successfully after two and a half months, the effects of this situation have continued to have an impact on the contract with reference to cashflow, resourcing the works, performance of sub-contractors etc.

As stated above, the approved design meant that floor levels on the lower ground floor and external ground levels were to be dropped considerably—up to four metres in front of the house. To achieve this, it was necessary to underpin extensive parts of the building to lower the bearing point of foundations. This is a very slow and painstaking process which was greatly exacerbated by substantial ground water and most critically, a spring at the middle of the north elevation which had washed out the mortar from the masonry wall over time. Secant piling was used to retain the ground in front of the house along Oakley Road where the deepest excavation was needed. It was also necessary to install rock anchors in this area to prevent the new construction from floating due to the high water table.

As work proceeded and the existing house was stripped and underpinning was proceeding, it was discovered that the basic structure was in quite poor condition. Among the difficulties encountered that had to be addressed was insufficient bonding between walls at right angles to each other which necessitated the casting in of reinforced concrete elbows. The base of the north wall and the main flue stack were both in unacceptably poor condition which resulted in the need for needling and propping the walls above and the replacement of substantial areas of them up to ground floor level. There was also a need to strengthen all the suspended floors and to tie them more securely to the walls. Stability of the north elevation became a major concern during underpinning and it had to be extensively propped using temporary shoring. When the external walls were stripped it was found that there were extensive timber elements built in, which had to

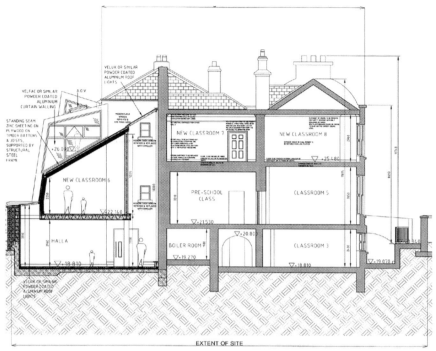

Architect's plan showing the north-south section—the view from Scoil Bhríde—indicating how the new extension fits in with the original house.

be removed and the walls repaired.

The main chimney stack was in poor shape, especially the sand cement plaster. When this was removed it was found to be necessary to re-build the whole chimney. The works also include extensive drainage work including the picking up of the drainage from No. 21 Oakley Road. As we have lowered the floor below gravity drainage level, a pumping system with associated sumps for both foul and surface water are incorporated. During the works, it was found that substantial surface water was entering the site from Scoil Bhríde. This had to be intercepted and a new drain out to the street run along the south boundary.

All these difficulties discovered during the works have created extensive additional work and associated costs. Each item had to be addressed, costed and Departmental approval sought before it could proceed. This process, despite speedy responses from the Department, as well as the amount of additional works, created a need to extend the contract period for the works from 13 months to almost 24 months.

The examinership of Dunne Contracting Ltd has also created challenges related to cashflow and credit lines which have affected progress of the works. Due to difficulties being encountered by the contractor, there were significant changes of key site personnel during the contract which exacerbated matters further.

It should be noted that the refurbishment and extension of Cullenswood House was always going to be very challenging due to the very restricted nature of the site, difficult access off Oakley Road, the very poor condition of the house and the extremely challenging ground conditions. These challenges were greatly increased by the financial difficulties encountered by the contractor. It must be acknowledged that the project would never have proceeded without the vision and imagination of the Department of Education and Science.

Notwithstanding the difficulties, the completed project will provide unique accommodation for Lios na nÓg on this historic site which is steeped in heritage and history. It is hoped that the works have respected and enhanced the heritage and protected this historic building well into the future and that the newly accommodated school will extend this building and site's long historical association with education at the forefront of innovation.

Above: the renovated first floor classroom.
Below: the renovated ground floor classroom.

The Celtic Revival wallpaper:
A report by David Skinner Wallpapers

Wallpaper of a Celtic design still hung in the upstairs landing of Cullenswood House when the refurbishment work began. We were unable to find out anything very conclusive about the date and the origin of the paper. The way the coloured inks are applied appears to indicate that the paper was machine printed, rather than hand-block printed. (However, it is impossible to be totally definite even about this.) Machine-printed wallpapers were in widespread use from the mid-19th century onwards.

The fact that the paper is probably machine printed suggests that it was a mass-produced pattern, rather than a one-off commission.

Celtic Revival motifs are very rare in wallpapers and it has not been possible to find anything similar to this pattern in any of the published material. It is not possible to establish whether English manufacturers would have considered the market for Celtic Revival motifs significant enough to put a pattern such as this into production. If it is a machine-printed paper, then it is possible that it was printed by the firm of Coxons, who had a wallpaper factory in Bray which closed down in the 1960s or 1970s. Attempts to get in touch with former staff of Coxons were unsuccessful.

All that can be said about the paper is:
- It could date from any time between the late 19th century and the 1970s.
- It is probably machine printed, but just may be hand printed. Examination by someone more expert may possibly help to determine this. Analysis of the pigments might be of help.
- Further research is needed to find out whether it might have been produced by Coxons of Bray, or possibly by an English manufacturer.

With this in mind, it was decided that the best way forward was to preserve at least one representative length intact, to allow for further research to be undertaken. A section of the wallpaper was carefully removed by David Skinner at the start of the works and preserved. It will be reinstated on site in the same location and protected to preserve it from potential future damage.

A patch of the old wallpaper found on the upstairs landing during the renovation.

Ag foghlaim i dTeach Fhíodh Cuillinn: Lios na nÓg amárach agus feasta

Gréagóir Ó Dúill

Fearann beag talaimh is ea Raghnallach i ndeisceart Bhaile Átha Cliath. Cuma Ghaelach ar an ainm, ach is deacair a bheith cinnte an Gaelach atá sé, ar baisteadh as Ranelagh Gardens London é, nó a mhalairt. Creidim go bhfuil teorainneacha nádúrtha ag an bhfearann bheag sin, mar a bhíonn ag limistéir fholláin: an Dothair ó dheas, an Chanáil Mhór ó thuaidh, an N11, mórbhealach an oirdheiscirt thoir agus abhainn bheag an Swan, croí Rath Maonais nó líne an Luais Ghlais thiar.

Istigh sa cheantar bheag seo, is iomaí rud spéisiúil a thit amach agus a thiteann amach go fóill. Sampla fíochmhar díobh ionsaí tobann mhuintir Ghaelach Bhranach na sléibhte ar chathróirí Bhaile Átha Cliath agus iad ag picniceáil i bhFeadh Cuillinn ag tarraingt ar ocht gcéad bliain ó shin. Ach d'imigh an lá sin. Sampla eile, sampla aerach, an balún a thug Richard Crosbie in airde spéire ó ghairdíní Raghnallach, an chéad eitilt os cionn na hÉireann agus aer te á iompar—b'álainn an radharc aige ar chuar na bá móire ó Bhré go Binn Éadair, radharc nach raibh ag éinne roimhe ach a bhíonn againn féin go minic, muid ag teacht isteach chun tuirlingt san aerphort.

Maireann an bua sin i Raghnallach i gcónaí. Tá Gaelscoil Lios na nÓg ina shampla eile. Thosaigh an Ghaelscoil ar an chúis is simplí—ní raibh oideachas ar fáil do bhuíon páistí mar a d'iarr a dtuismitheoirí agus chinneadar é a chur ar fáil. 'Is féidir linn.' Ní raibh áit acu don scoil, agus chuadar chucu sin a bhí i gceannas ar cheann de na hinstitiúidí ba thábhachtaí sa tír ó thaobh stair an oideachais de, agus tugadh bheith istigh dóibh. Níor de thaisme an t-iarratas, níor de thaisme an fáilte nó is ionann, cuid mhaith aidhmeanna na dtuismitheoirí bunaidh sin agus aidhmeanna na hinstitúide seanbhunaithe, Teach Fhíodh Cuillinn, Scoil Éanna an Phiarsaigh.

Tá an chéad ghlúin de pháistí Lios na nÓg ar tí an mheánscoil a fhágáil anois, iad ina mná óga agus ina bhfir óga déanta, chun aghaidh a thabhairt ar shaol mór na hoibre, ar an oideachas tríú leibhéal, ar an imirce féin gach seans, ar shaol an duine aibí fhásta. Féadaimid bheith cinnte gur láidre, gur sciliúla, gur neamhspleáí iad de thairbe a gcuid blianta bunscolaíochta ar Lios na nÓg. Agus an bhuíon tuismitheoirí ag teacht le chéile—i lár na sráide i gcéaduair, ansin i seomra suite, i dtolglann tí ósta, i halla chumann leadóige de réir mar a d'fhás na huimhreacha—bhí rudaí ann nár ghá a phlé. Go mbeadh idir ghasúir agus ghirseacha ann le chéile sa scoil. Gur teagasc tré Ghaeilge a thabharfaí. Go mbeadh bainistíocht na scoile faoi na tuismitheoirí. Go mbeadh pobal na scoile ina choincheap beo agus aidhm aige an timpeallacht chultúrtha uilig a shaibhriú. Gur scoil bheag mhaith a bhí a dhíth orthu. Chuireadar chuige.

Agus an chéad ghlúin sin ag dul chun cinn, is mithid a aithint gur scaipeadar cheana. Mar is dual, chaitheadar a mblianta meánscoile i scoileanna éagsúla, nó is mór le muintir Lios na nÓg an éagsúlacht. Chuadar ar scoileanna éagsúla sa cheantar, ag cur le caighdeán Gaeilge na ranganna ina raibh siad, gníomhach sna díospóireachtaí agus sna himeachtaí éagsúla Gaeilge agus eile, ag mealladh cairde le tréimhse a chaitheamh sna coláistí samhraidh sa Ghaeltacht agus mar sin—gaoiste i dtaos mheánscolaíocht dheisceart Bhaile Átha Cliath, idir scoileanna lánGhaelacha agus scoileanna eile. Duine nó beirt, thug a dtuismitheoirí leo iad chuig réigiúin eile den tír, ag filleadh ar an dúchas tuaithe nó ag tapú deise. Tá, cheana, tréimhsí fada caite ag dornán duine díobh thar lear, iad ag foghlaim na beatha idirnáisiúnaí sin atá ag teacht chugainn, beatha idirnáisiúnta a raibh a mblianta i Lios na nÓg ina oiliúint mhaith di.

Athraíonn an saol. Athraíonn Raghnallach. Ceantar de sheomraí cónluí a bhíodh ann i seascaidí na haoise seo caite, sna seachtóidí féin, daonra mór de mhic léinn, de bhanaltraí agus d'ógstátseirbhísigh, ceantar gan scoil pharóiste. De réir a chéile, bhog teaghlaigh ar ais isteach ann agus méadaíodh an gá le scoileanna—b'shin fáth bhunú na scoile mar ba chúis freisin í le bunú scoil idirchreidmheach Raghnallach trátha an ama chéanna. I mblianta na hinimirce, tháining méadú ar líon na ndaoine sa cheantar a rugadh thar lear, daoine nárbh eagal leo tabhairt faoin dara, faoin tríú, faoin ceathrú teanga agus thug cuid acu sin a gcuid páistí i gcúram Lios na nÓg. Tógadh cuid mhór tithe agus árasán sa cheantar nuair a aithníodh chomh dúilmhear agus a bhíonn daoine a bheith gar don chathair, gar don Luas agus mar sin, gan a saol a mheilt ar an taisteal laethúil. Is daoine iad seo a raibh fonn ar chuid shuntasach acu lámh ghníomhach a bheith acu in oideachas a bpáistí, daoine a bhí in ann droichead a thógáil gan eagla idir an t-idirnáisiúnachas agus an cultúr Gaelach, idir an traidisiún agus an nua-aois. Thuigeadar na buntáistí a bhaineann le dhá arm aigne, leis an dátheangachas sin a chothaíonn cumas anailíse agus roghnaithe duine óig. Thuigeadar nach áit bhreithe an teist ar dhuine, ar mhúinteoir a d'fhás aníos i gcomhluadar Gaeltachta nó ar dhuine óg cathrach ar thoradh é ar chóras Gaelscolaíochta na cathrach (ar dheacair de ghnáth aithint eatarthu ar na saolta seo). Ná nach ceart ach an oiread deighilt a dhéanamh idir leanbh as tír eile agus leanbh de phór na nDubs. D'aithin siad go raibh gá leanúnach le hobair—leis an Ghaeilge a choinneáil in uachtar (sainmharc indibhidiúil na scoile), leis an fhéinmhuinín a chothú i measc phobal na scoile agus i measc na bpáistí ach go háirithe.

Na tuismitheoirí bunaidh sin nach raibh aon tslí dá gcuid páistí ina gceantar féin, agus go raibh orthu scoil a bhunú dóibh féin, d'fhoghlaim siad gur ceart a bheith fáiltiúil oscailte. Tagann cuid mhór as sin— ina measc bua Lios na nÓg sa tionscnamh náisiúnta idirchultúrtha 'Building for the Future—Caring for Others', tionscnamh a bhunaigh Lios ar dhúchas na dtuismitheoirí as tíortha eile i 2003 inar bhuaigh an scoil €25,000. D'fhoghlaim na tuismitheoirí, mar a bhí a fhios ag an phríomhoide a ceapadh, Áine Nic an tShíthigh, gur ceart oiread agus is féidir a chur isteach i saol an dalta gan é a phlúchadh. An curaclam agus an siollabas, ar ndóigh—is bunscoil, nó scoil náisiúnta atá i Lios na nÓg, agus an Roinn Oideachais agus Eolaíochta ag déanamh cúraim di, ina barántas ar bhunchaighdeáin, ag cinntiú an mhaoinithe. Ach déanann na múinteoirí agus na tuismitheoirí cuid mhór a shocrú sa bhreis air sin—cuairteanna aonuaire cosúil leis an chuairt a rinne P. J. Lynch, maisitheoir clúiteach leabhar, an cúrsa de sheisiúin agus de cheardlanna a rinne Áine Ní Ghlinn, scríbhneoir, na cúrsaí i scileanna drámaíochta ag Ray Yeates, na turasanna ar dhánlanna agus iarsmalanna agus láithreachta oidhreachta—baineann Cill Maighneann go mór leis an scéal seo—na cuairteanna a dhéanann tuismitheoirí as tíortha eile chun a ndúchas agus a nósmhaireacht féin a léiriú do pháistí Lios na nÓg. Féach gur cumas an linbh í féin a chur in iúl is cuspóir do chuid mhór díobh seo.

Mar chuid de fhís na mbunaitheoirí, mar chuid den chomhréiteach a rinneadar leo sin a bhí mar iontaobhaithe agus caomhnóirí ag Teach Fhíodh Cuillinn, tá aitheantas soiléir ann gurb áis agus acmhainn chultúrtha ag pobal iomlán na scoile, ag pobal an cheantair, ag pobal Gaeilge dheisceart na cathrach atá i nGaelscoil Lios na nÓg. Bíonn agus beidh ocáidí rialta ar siúl chun cur le gréasán tacaíochta na scoile agus an chultúir tré chéile—ranganna agus seisiúin, seimineáir agus ciorcail chaidrimh, grúpaí sóisialta de gach saghas. Gníomhaíonn an scoil mar a bheadh lár-ionad teacht le chéile agus fócas ag daltaí, ag tuismitheoirí, ag iardhaltaí agus ag iarthuismitheoirí, ag daoine eile nach bhfuil de nasc acu leis an scoil ach an nasc sin is tábhachtaí, spéis i ngnéithe éagsúla an chultúir dhúchais agus i leas na leanaí. Agus imríonn tionchar dá réir ar an cheantar thart timpeall—ar an Ranelagh Arts Festival, ar an togra Lá Geal Gréine agus mar sin de.

Tá, gan amhras, a n-áit féin ag an cheol agus ag an sport i measc na ngnéithe cultúrtha seo, taobh istigh d'am na scoile agus taobh amuigh de, i modh comortais mar a bhíonn an pheil agus an iománaíocht, nó ar mhaithe le páirt a ghlacadh agus sásamh a bhaint as caighdeán ard a bhaint amach, faoi mar a dhéantar i gCórFhéile na Scol. Cuidíonn sé gur cinneadh i dtosach báire an scoil a choinneáil beag agus maith, gan ach an t-aon rang páistí a scaoileadh isteach gach fómhar, cuid mhaith acu sin ó Naíonra Lios na nÓg nó/ agus ina ndeartháireacha nó ina ndeirfiúracha ag daltaí atá sa scoil cheana féin. Sin bealach a chinntíonn go leanann *ethos* na scoile ar aghaidh ó bhliain go chéile, ag freagairt don lá inniu, don lá amárach, agus ag déanamh forbartha i gcónaí ar fhís na mbunaitheoirí.

Teach Fhíodh Cuillinn, is teach í a thugann fianaise ar an oidhreacht Sheoirseach sin ba thabhartas ailtireachta a tugadh do mhuintir na hÉireann. Ba theach sean-athair William Lecky é, staraí an ochtú céad déag, a d'oibrigh amach conas a gceart a thabhairt do stair na n-aicmí éagsúla in Éirinn go liobrálach fírinneach cothrom. Is teach é inar fhéach Pádraig Mac Piarais le fíorú a dhéanamh ar theoiricí agus ar chleachtais an oideachais dhátheangaigh, ar Mhodh Gouin mar ar tháinig sé air sa Bheilg agus é ag déanamh taighde, deich mbliana sular chuimhnigh an Réamonnach ar fhuil a dhoirteadh ar son '*gallant little Belgium*'. Timpeallacht shaibhir fhiúntach. Ní bhíonn mórán de chur amach ag páistí ar thaibhsí na staire, ach an mhuintir óga a oibríonn go dícheallach sa tseomra ranga, a thógann callán na saoirse sa chlós, bíonn siad ag athscríobh na staire, ag athshealbhú oidhreachta luachmhair, ag déanamh cinnte den todhchaí—agus ag baint taitnimh as an tsaol.

Education in Cullenswood House:
Lios na nÓg into the future

Gréagóir Ó Dúill

Ranelagh, in south Dublin, is a small area. The name looks Gaelic in origin, but one cannot be sure it is in fact Gaelic, or whether it was called after Ranelagh Gardens in London—or vice versa. I think this little urban area has natural borders, as a healthy specific area should: the Dodder meanders on the southern boundary, the Grand Canal runs straight along the northern side, the N11, motorway to the southeast and the little lost river of the Swan in Rathmines to the west, or, in today's times, the Green Line of the Luas tramway.

Within this little area many interesting things have happened and still happen. A ferocious example was the sudden raid by the Gaelic O'Tooles and Byrnes of the Wicklow mountains on the burghers of Dublin as they picnicked at Feighcullen woods, almost 800 years ago. But that day is over. More recently, and more happily, Richard Crosbie made the first hot air balloon ascent in Ireland from Ranelagh—he enjoyed the view of the sweep of Dublin Bay from Bray to Howth not seen before from above by anyone, but which we enjoy often, our plane descending to the airport as we come gladly home.

Ranelagh still has interesting things to record. Gaelscoil Lios na nÓg is an example. The gaelscoil started up for the simplest, the most valid of reasons—the kind of education their parents wanted for them was just not available for all the children in the area, so they decided to make it available. 'Yes, we can. *Is féidir linn*.'

They had no site for a school and they went to those who had the powers of decision over one of the most important institutions in the educational history of the country and were given a welcome. The approach was no accident, the welcome was no accident, for the aims of those founding parents were very close to the aims of the

In the old playground.

old-established institution, Cullenswood House, the founding place of Pearse's Scoil Éanna.

The first generation of Lios na nÓg pupils is on the point of leaving secondary school soon, young men and women, looking forward to facing the life of work and responsibility, of third level education, perhaps of migration, the life of the mature grown adult. We can be sure that they are stronger, more skilled in life's needs, more independent because of their years of primary education in Lios na nÓg. And that group of parents who came together—at first in the middle of the road, then in a sitting room, then in a hotel lounge, then, as their numbers grew, in a tennis club hall—they worked together because there were things which were given, on which they did not have to speak.

That both boys and girls would attend the school. That teaching would be through Irish. That the parents themselves would take on the management of the school. That the concept of the school community would be alive and strong, that it would hope to spread out and enrich the wider cultural environment. That the school would not be too big, but would concentrate on being a good school. They worked towards those ends.

As this first generation progressed onward and outward, we should admit that they are already scattered. They went on to different secondary schools, since the Lios na nÓg people value difference, independence, choice. In those schools they enhanced the level of spoken Irish in their class and outside it, and took part in activities such as debates, and formed little nuclei which went to Gaeltacht summer colleges, bringing their friends, and so on—a natural yeast in the dough of the secondary schools of south Dublin, whether Irish medium or not. One or two went with their parents to live in other parts of the country, returning to a rural background or following a dream or seizing an opportunity. A couple of them have already spent lengthy periods abroad, learning that international life which is so important to their generation, an international life for which their years in Lios na nÓg were a fine preparation.

Life changes. Ranelagh changes. In the 1960s and into the 1970s, it was an area of flats and bedsitting rooms with a large and fluctuating population of students, of nurses and young civil servants. It was an area with no parish school. Gradually, families moved in and the need for schools became apparent. This was the reason for the founding of Lios na nÓg as it was for the founding, at much the same time, of Ranelagh Multi-Denominational School. In the years of large-scale immigration, the number of the people in the area who had been born abroad increased sharply, often people quite happy to take on the third or fourth language, people who saw multiculturalism as natural and advantageous to their children. Some of them gave their children to the care of Lios na nÓg.

Many new apartment blocks and houses were built in the area, as the advantages became obvious of living close to the city, to the Luas line, within walking or cycling distance of work and the developed facilities of the city. Many of these young parents wanted to have an active part in their children's education, and were quite happy that there is a natural bridge between Irish medium education and the multicultural multilingual future, that tradition and modernity are as natural allies as Irish and English, the two languages operating together. They knew that birthplace is not the measure of a person, whether that is another parent, or a teacher who may have grown up in a rural Gaeltacht community or perhaps in the city, benefitting from a Gaelscoil network already in place. So there was no reason to differentiate between a child born abroad and a young Dub. The parents recognised that there was and always would be need for effort—to keep up the Irish language (the individual characteristic of the school), to encourage self-confidence in the school community and especially among the children.

The founding parents who had learned that there was no room for their children in the existing provision of Irish language education in the area, so had gone on to found their own school, learned, too, that they, in turn, should actively welcome others, be open. Much comes of that. One example is the success of Lios na nÓg in the national multiculturalism project and competition 'Building for the Future—Caring for Others', a project based in Lios on the diverse cultural background of the parents of the school in 2003 which won the school €25,000. The parents learned, as the first principal, Áine Nic an tShíthigh, was aware, that the child's life should be enriched by diversity, by experience. The curriculum and syllabus of the Department of Education and Science underpins and provides a framework for the school's work, as the Department warrants the standards, and provides the bulk of the funding for the school.

But the teachers and the parents make many arrangements over and above those basics. Examples include the one-off visits such as that by P. J. Lynch, famous illustrator of children's books, the course of sessions and workshops in creative writing by Áine Ní Ghlinn, writer, the courses in drama skills by Ray Yeates, visits to galleries, to museums, to heritage sites (and of course Kilmainham is one of these). Other examples are the well-established visits by parents from other cultures bringing in a taste of their own national culture. The aim of much of this activity is to deepen each child's capacity to understand and to express.

The founders' original vision for the school was at one with that of the Cullenswood House Restoration Committee, who acted as its guardians and restorers before the foundation of Lios. They agreed that the school should operate as a cultural resource centre for the whole school community, for the surrounding community, for the Irish language community of south Dublin. Regular and frequent social occasions occur to reinforce the support network both of the school and of the culture—classes and sessions, workshops and seminars, social groups and conversation circles of all kinds. The school acts as a centre for people to come together, as a focus for students and ex-students, parents and ex-parents, and people who have no connection with the school other than the most important, an interest in an aspect of Irish culture and in the welfare of the children. And so the school operates its influence naturally on the surrounding area, on, say, the Ranelagh Arts Festival or the Irish conversation project Lá Geal Gréine.

Of course, music and sport are a part of the school's life and the life of the children, both in school hours and outside of them. Sometimes, as with football, this takes the form of participation in competitions. At other times, as in the case of the schools choral festival, the participation is aimed at enjoyment and reaching a high standard. The initial decision to keep the school small and at a high standard is relevant to these activities, as only one reception class is formed each autumn and only a small number of pupils can be admitted. Many of these come from the Naíonra attached to the school, others are brothers and sisters of existing pupils. This ensures that the ethos of the school continues from year to year, while always conscious of the founders' vision and the day-to-day needs of the current school population.

Cullenswood House is a fine example of Georgian architecture which is part of the common heritage of this country, and especially of this city. It belonged to the grandfather of the historian Lecky, who worked in the 19th century on the history of the 18th, endeavouring to treat equally the differing classes and traditions of the Irish people and to do that in a way which was truthful, liberal, generous. It is a house in which Patrick Pearse attempted to develop and bring to fruition the theories of bilingual education, particularly the Gouin Method which he had encountered in Belgium when he researched the issue of teaching young people in an environment of two languages. That was ten years before Redmond discovered 'gallant little Belgium' and invited young Irishmen to join in the war of the trenches.

Cullenswood House is a rich environment. Primary school children have limited interest in the ghosts of the past. But those young people who work hard in their classrooms, who celebrate their freedom in the schoolyard, they are practising the revision of history, they are repossessing a valuable heritage, they are ensuring the future. They are enjoying life.

The contributors

Róisín de Buitléar is an artist and one of the founders of Lios na nÓg. Her sculptural work is in private and public collections in Ireland and abroad. Her commissioned work can be seen in public buildings throughout Ireland including the Visitors' Centre in Dún Chaoin, Kerry, National Museums of Northern Ireland, Belfast, the National Botanic Gardens, Dublin and the National Museum of Ireland collection. She has lectured worldwide and published numerous articles on contemporary Irish glass.

Deirdre Donnelly trained at the Abbey School of Acting and was a member of the Abbey Company for some years. She has worked as an actress in Ireland for the past 37 years.

Paddy Fletcher is currently Joint Managing Director of A & D Wejchert. His work has been related to educational and commercial buildings as well as a number of private houses. His main interests are sustainability and low energy design—he was Partner in charge of the Waterford Institute of Technology Library, which won the Minister for Environment's Sustainability 2000 Award. He was also in charge of the Waterford Institute of Technology Nurse Education Building which was awarded the Department of Environment, Heritage and Local Government Sustainability Award, 2007, and the Royal Institute of the Architects of Ireland Best Sustainable Project, 2007. He is involved with the successful consortium which won the PPP Schools Bundle 1 in Ireland which has just started on site. He is a member of the RIAI Competence Task Force.

Alan Gilsenan is an award-winning film-maker, writer and theatre director. His films include: *The Road To God Knows Where*, *All Souls' Day*, *Zulu 9*, *The Green Fields of France*, *The Ghost of Roger Casement*, *Timbuktu*, *The Dark School* and *The Yellow Bittern* as well as the acclaimed documentary series *The Asylum*, *The Hospice*, *The Irish Mind* and *I See A Darkness*.

For the theatre, he has directed his own adaptation of John Banville's *The Book of Evidence*, Tom Murphy's *The Patriot Game*, Tom MacIntyre's *What Happened Bridgie Cleary*, Jean Genet's *The Balcony*, Tennessee Williams's *Small Craft Warnings* and Samuel Beckett's *Footfalls*. Gilsenan has a long-standing interest in Patrick Pearse and is directing a major theatre piece inspired by his life and artistic writings.

Deirdre Kelly, who died in 2000, was a lifelong advocate for her native Dublin, its history, its architecture and its people. A graduate of the National College of Art, then in Kildare Street, she worked in a pottery, at the National Museum and then as an art teacher in Inchicore Vocational School. As a mature student she studied history and archaeology at University College, Dublin. She was a co-founder, in 1972, of the Living City Group which ran public exhibitions and meetings to fight against the depopulation of the inner city. She joined the Old Dublin Society, An Taisce, the Irish Georgian Society and the Dublin Civic Group. She helped organise the three-day Dublin Crisis Conference in 1986 which eventually led to the repopulation of the inner city. In 1996 she was appointed to the Architectural Committee of the Heritage Council which she attended until her illness in 1999. In June 2000 Dublin Corporation established an annual conservation bursary in memory of Deirdre Kelly. In 2009 a memorial to Kelly, in the form of a replica of her much-loved bicycle in a box submerged in the pavement, was installed by Dublin City Council in the Triangle, Ranelagh.

Éilis Ní Dhuibhne was born in 1954. She is a writer in both Irish and English. Her novels include *The Dancers Dancing, Fox Swallow Scarecrow, Dúnmharú sa Daingean, Hurlamaboc,* and many others. She has won several awards for her writing and is a member of Aosdána. She worked for many years as a curator in the National Library and currently teaches on the MA in Creative Writing in UCD. She attended Scoil Bhríde from 1959 to 1966.

Gréagóir Ó Dúill is a writer with eight collections of poetry published in Irish, a *Selected Poems*, two anthologies, a collection of short stories and a biography in Irish, and a collection in English; a director of *Comhar*, a founder of Lios na nÓg, a life vice-president of the Irish Labour History Society and honorary archivist of the Railway Records Society. He has lectured on creative writing in the Poets' House, Donegal, and in Waterford Institute of Technology, and on contemporary literature in Irish in Queen's University, Belfast.

Finola O'Kane is college lecturer in architecture and conservation at UCD. Her first book, *Landscape Design in Eighteenth-century Ireland: Mixing Foreign Trees with the Natives* was published in 2004 and awarded the inaugural J. B. Jackson Book Prize by the American Landscape Foundation in 2007. An architect, she has published widely on Irish design history both nationally and internationally, and is currently completing her second book entitled *Ireland and the Picturesque*. She co-edited a volume of essays entitled *Georgian Dublin* with Gillian O'Brien in 2008, and is also engaged in a study of nationalism and the Irish landscape which draws on her research into the landscape interests of Patrick Pearse. These were first addressed during her postgraduate studies at the Architectural Association in London and published in 2000 as 'Nurturing a Revolution—Patrick Pearse's School Garden at St. Enda's' in the *Journal of the Garden History Society*.

Peter Pearson is a painter and architectural historian. Among his best-selling books have been *Dublin's Victorian Houses*, *Between the Mountains and the Sea* and *Decorative Dublin*. As an activist with An Taisce and the Dublin Civic Trust he was instrumental in the conservation of many historic buildings in Dublin, including Drimnagh Castle. His painting is hugely inspired by Dublin's built heritage.

Ruairí Quinn TD, architect and planner, is Labour Party Spokesperson for Education and Science. He has a deep interest in urban and planning affairs which he has written about in his memoir *Straight Left: A Journey in Politics*.

Elaine Sisson is the IADT Fellow at the Graduate School of Creative Arts and Media, Dublin. She was previously Senior Lecturer in Visual Culture at IADT, Dún Laoghaire, lecturing across programmes including visual communications, fine art, production design, and animation. She wrote a book on the cultural history of Patrick Pearse's school for boys, St Enda's, entitled *Pearse's Patriots* which was published by Cork University Press in 2004. She is co-editing a collection of essays on Irish design and material culture called *Made in Ireland? Visualising Modernity : 1922–1992*. Her current research interests are focused on uncovering radical and bohemian cultural life in Ireland during the 1920s and 1930s.

Victoria White has 20 years' experience as a writer and editor, including five years as Arts Editor of *The Irish Times*. She has had a lifelong interest in Irish language, folklore and song and has been active in organising many cultural events in Cullenswood House. She is also an environmental activist, being co-founder of Dublin Friends of the Earth.

INDEX

INDEX